WHEN GOD
FEELS FAR AWAY

*A Personal, Practical Guide to
Overcoming the Spiritual Traps that
Keep You from Drawing Closer to God*

DEBBIE MASCIOLI

Unless noted, Scriptures are taken from the NEW AMERICAN STANDARD BIBLE®, Copyright © 1960, 1962, 1963, 1968, 1971, 1972, 1973, 1975, 1977, 1995 by The Lockman Foundation. Used by permission.

Scripture quotations marked NKJV are taken from the New King James Version®. Copyright © 1982 by Thomas Nelson. Used by permission. All rights reserved.

Scripture quotations marked KJV are taken from the KING JAMES VERSION (KJV): KING JAMES VERSION, public domain.

Scripture quotations marked NIV are taken from THE HOLY BIBLE, NEW INTERNATIONAL VERSION®, NIV® Copyright © 1973, 1978, 1984, 2011 by Biblica, Inc.® Used by permission. All rights reserved worldwide.

Visit the author's website at www.debbiemascioli.com

Printed in the United States of America

Mascioli, Debbie.
When God Feels Far Away: A Personal, Practical Guide to Overcoming the Spiritual Traps that Keep You From Drawing Closer to God / Debbie Mascioli.
pages cm
ISBN 978-0-692-95001-2
1. Meditation—Prayer—Being Still—Hearing God—
Christianity—Empowerment I. Title.

First Edition
10 9 8 7 6 5 4 3 2 1

CONTENTS

This book
is dedicated
as a humble
offering of
love to my Lord and Savior. What the Holy Spirit has taught me
firsthand is shown in the following pages; It comes through
life experiences He has given to me. Through growth and
understanding,
wisdom and
awareness,
discernment
and power,
evidence

of His

presence,
w i t h
encouraging
w o r d s,

He has
equipped
me to share
truth with
you, His
Beloved.

PREFACE

This book is a tool to help you, the reader, come to see what holds you back from having a deeper, more fulfilling relationship with God.

I offer this personal, practical guide from my life lessons. It is certainly not an exhaustive tool to serve this topic. It is, however, perfect for those who desire a closer walk with the Lord. It offers easy, practical suggestions to get you started.

Spiritual traps paralyze us and keep us from pressing in as we desire more of God. I expose a few of these traps, such as busyness, an overactive mind, and a religious spirit, in hopes it will bring understanding to the struggles you may have in your life. This will help you escape the trap and embrace your relationship with God.

Does God feel far away? Many of us grope in the darkness trying to fill a void, to make ourselves happy, or feel satisfied. We try to fill this void with everything but God. Ultimately, everything outside of God is counterfeit.

If you are committed and diligent to applying the basic biblical principles found in this book, your life will never be the same again. Allow my personal stories to inspire you. But most of all, may the Word of God reign powerfully in your life. Follow hard after Him!

"God feels far away" is a statement many people use during different seasons of their lives. The next book in the *When God Feels Far Away* series will be a personal, practical guide to overcoming difficult circumstances.

God often feels far away when we have been personally responsible for an action or decision that ends with unfavorable results. Sometimes it's due to someone else's actions, whether through intent or neglect. How do we manage to get through these circumstances?

These questions, and more, will be answered throughout the pages of the next book in this series. Visit my author page, **Debbie Mascioli, Author**, on Facebook for news and updates.

ACKNOWLEDGEMENTS

I am a follower of Jesus-Wife-Mom-Friend-Coach-Author.

Father, you are my Daddy.
Jesus, you are my Redeemer.
Holy Spirit, you are my gift.

My husband Sammy, you are my soulmate.
Katie-Lynn, Sammy, Kelsey, and Solomon
My four precious children, you are my sunshine.
My friends, you are my inspiration.

My readers, you are my motivation.

I am so grateful for my sweet friends who came alongside me
to be the extra eyes and counsel to make this book come alive.

They say it takes a village to raise a child.
It takes a team to write a book.
My faithful and loving friends, I couldn't have done it without you.
Jen, you are the bomb at administration.
You helped the vision and saw it through to the end.
Thank you!

The Lord is good.

INTRODUCTION

For centuries, stories have been told about explorers searching for the great secret—the Fountain of Youth. Great men and women have spent lifetimes and lots of money trying, and failing, to find such a fountain. Similarly, many people search for the greatest *secret* of all—the secret to a close relationship with God. How does one have a close walk with God when He feels so far away? Unlike the unattainable Fountain of Youth, you can discover the secret to a closer walk with God by applying the principles in this book.

We get caught up in spiritual traps designed to create distance between us and God. This results in the lack of a meaningful relationship between God and His people. This book will expose some of these traps. It will provide the insight to help you escape them so you can embrace your relationship with God.

Many of us are groping in the darkness, searching for answers, wondering what plans God has for us. Do you feel stuck? Do you sense you're not hearing Him quite clearly? Maybe you've been serving Him faithfully and it doesn't seem like enough. If this resonates with you, this may be the book for you. It's filled with biblical principles that have been extremely effective in my own life and journey with the Lord.

Many people want God to move on their behalf. They ask the Lord to guide them and speak to them clearly, then wonder why they don't hear from Him. Yet when asked how much time they spend in quiet time with God, the majority say, "I don't. I'm too busy." They don't even realize that God is no longer a priority in their lives.

How do we expect to see God move, how do we overcome, when our hearts are positioned so far away from Him? Are you tired of feeling empty and alone? I believe many of us have struggled to maintain our relationship with God at some point in our lives. We hear exciting testimonies from people who walk closely with the Lord and have personally experienced His power in their lives. Have you thought these experiences were for everyone else but you? Why would you think that? They are for everyone who desires a close walk with the Lord.

The Bible is a powerful book that sets us free from sin and darkness when we apply its principles. James 4:7,8 (KJV) says, "Submit yourselves therefore to God. Resist the devil, and he will flee from you. Draw nigh to God, and He will draw nigh to you."

The distractions of this world are depleting our lives, keeping us from fully living as God intended us to live. Spiritual traps are an epidemic amongst God's people. They entice us and keep us from drawing closer to God.

Spiritual traps create loneliness, a lack of peace, and a level of anxiety or depression. They delay us from receiving the answers we desire. This book will help to expose some of these traps, but it is by no means an exhaustive list.

I pray you will begin to recognize for yourself some of the many additional spiritual traps Satan uses against you on your journey with Jesus. I strongly believe that by remaining stuck in these traps, you unknowingly forfeit your right to a closer walk with Him. If you struggle with obstacles in your life, pray as you read this book. Ask God to help you identify and overcome any traps that might be holding you captive.

This book was birthed from two desires: to point others to the heart of Jesus and to provide proven biblical principles to those who desire more. I hope you gain new insight as you read through the biblical principles and key verses that have been selected. I pray some of the experiences that have blessed me will inspire you to develop your own special time with the Lord. May you come to understand and know God in a much greater way. There's so much to learn of the vastness of God. Who could know it all? He promises if we seek Him, we will find Him. Let's seek Him together.

My prayer is that you will find what you are looking for, too. Are you ready? I'm excited! Let's go!

And you will seek Me and find Me, when
you search for me with all your heart.

Jeremiah 29:13

CHAPTER 1

CAUGHT IN THE SPIRITUAL TRAP

As leaves swirled across my lawn on a beautiful, sunny, fall afternoon, I received a call from a dear friend asking me to join her for lunch. We made plans to meet the next day. I thought she wanted to talk about a rough experience she was going through. I would soon discover that I couldn't have been more wrong.

We met at a diner, exchanging a warm hug and smiles. As the hostess led us to our table, I could tell that something was heavy on my friend's heart. I started to worry, wondering if she was okay. We made small talk first, ordered our meals, and then . . . the bombshell.

My friend shared her story: years of busy church activity had left her burned out, overwhelmed by life, and disconnected from people. Life circumstances had left a deep scar on her heart. I sat and listened, empathizing with her situation. My heart broke for my friend; I wanted so much more for her. I was puzzled. How had she stayed stuck so long? I couldn't begin to comprehend either the magnitude of the trial she had suffered or the negative repercussions. I was at a loss for words, so I asked a few questions in order to better understand her situation. As she answered, the real reason for the lunch invitation unfolded.

My sweet friend, whom I admire and love deeply, was gravely concerned for my personal well-being. She shared that the Holy Spirit had impressed upon her to speak with me. She addressed my busyness: I was captain of several ministries, running night and day while our new church building was under construction, and I often opened and closed the doors for many nightly church activities. I also led women's Bible studies, weekly church movie nights, and other similar meetings. Beyond that, I made myself available at the drop of a hat for those who were in crisis or in need. I spent hours upon hours counseling on the phone, all while mothering three small children and homeschooling them at the same time. Outside the church, I worked for a direct in-home sales business and attended a community Christian women's group.

My friend was concerned that I would burn out like she did; that the hectic pace of life would catch up with me; that frustration and lack of energy would blindside me. She poured out her heart, relating her pains and struggles to my life. The expression on her face was one of compassion and great concern; she didn't want me to suffer the same end result that she had. I inhaled, sat back, and took it all in for less than a minute before . . .

I busted out laughing.

The mere idea of me burning out was a joke. I wasn't overwhelmed; I felt like I was thriving! I went on and on about my strengths through all of my busyness and how I felt as if I could still do more. I think I took her by surprise—or maybe I didn't. She knew my personality; she could have expected my reaction. I thanked her for loving me and told her how much I appreciated her concern. I reassured her that would never happen to me. On the contrary, I was doing just fine. I was considering adding even more to my already full plate and was excited about it.

Honestly, I didn't see where she was going with this conversation. I thought I was just stepping up and doing what was needed. I enjoyed working diligently! I was blinded to the reality of just how occupied I was. However, true to my friend's prediction, that busyness eventually caught up with me. I knew I was missing something. I spent years groping in the darkness, unfulfilled.[1]

---

[1] Job 12:25

I unknowingly left that lunch full of pride, arrogance, and self-reliance. I was independent from God. *My satisfaction was wrapped up in my performance.* My busyness and all of the great activities weren't enough to fill the deep void within me. I desperately prayed and fasted for more, but I had no idea what "more" looked like.

I was caught in a spiritual trap of busyness. *A spiritual trap captures you, incapacitates you, and keeps you from deepening your relationship with Jesus.* These traps come in all shapes and sizes, either suddenly or with a slow fade. The good old hamster wheel analogy shows just one example of a spiritual trap. We keep doing the same things over and over, expecting different results.

You probably picked up this book because you're a lot like me. Most of us desire more, much more than what we have now. We know something is missing. So we run around, trying to find what will satisfy this longing for more, all along missing the fact that a deeper relationship with God is what we truly hunger for. When He feels far away, we chase after counterfeits before we find that earthly pleasures will not satisfy us. The soul, a space only God can fill, longs for that which is spiritual and holy.

You might be thinking, "I have a relationship with the Lord. I'm doing well." I would counter, "That's great!" However, the vastness of God knows no limits. You cannot find His end or beginning. So much more is out there for you. Let's dig and explore the depths of God together.

In my life, the trap of busyness was reflected in my attitude through the harsh tone of my voice, constant rushing, lack of sleep, and a racing mind. My family suffered from this. Remember, I had three small children. I was in a whirlwind of out-of-control living with no idea how to make it all slow down, let alone stop.

Until I discovered the *secret* that really isn't a secret at all. For years, I searched for the secret to have a closer walk with the Lord. *I thought traveling the road of busyness was where I would find it.* I was doing all the "right" things, or so I thought. Yet I still felt like something was missing.

After my lunch date, the Lord started to work on me; my eyes were beginning to open. I began to pray. That's what we do, right? All I can say is, be prepared when you ask God for answers. He has a way of giving them to us in the most unusual ways. I believe He used my friend as a voice of reason to get my attention. He knew I wouldn't figure it out on my own. I was going too fast to hear Him.

I never would have expected the answer to come the way it did. It wasn't at all what I was looking for. It was, however, exactly what I needed. It wasn't until a year and a half later that my transformational journey to discovering more of God began.

The beginning of my personal journey

When I became pregnant with my fourth child a year later, my friend's prophecy came true. The stress finally caught up with me. As a result, I had to go on bed rest when I was five months pregnant. Even so, my son was born eleven weeks early, after just twenty-nine weeks of gestation. At 2.5 pounds and 19 inches, he needed to spend two heart-wrenching months in the Neonatal Intensive Care Unit.

After he was born, normal life came to a screeching halt. Everything changed. My world as I once knew it was no more. My daily routines, my friends, my church attendance, and outside ministry—done. I hit a brick wall. Loving friends chauffeured me back and forth to the hospital every day for 60 days. The Lord gave me a privileged bird's-eye view to what a small population of women and their families experience.

I had not been privy to this section of the hospital until then. My first few weeks in the NICU were stressful, upsetting, and nerve-wracking, with lots of ups and downs in my little son's life.

Once he was stabilized, I began to connect with other moms. I had come to find that not all moms were going home with their babies. The thought of leaving the hospital unable to take your baby home was devastating to me. I hated death. I hated watching moms mourn the loss of their children. Just recalling this as I type brings me to tears. It was a sad and traumatic time. I did not want to be a part of this. That experience is deep within my heart; it has changed me forever. All I can say is, "but God!" He chose me to be an encouragement and support for those in need. A new ministry started in the unlikeliest of places.

The Lord halted my busyness and took me to a new dimension of life in the most unusual way—sitting still. I sat in the NICU for over 8 hours each day, a mother bird watching over my chick. This is where He started training me. I read my Scriptures more than ever. I read them to my baby boy and memorized them. I sang and played worship songs for him. I journaled my prayers and God's answers. I fasted every week. God started to reveal a difference in the way I did life. I began talking to God about everything—even every single breath my son would take. I was now camped out at the Lord's throne of Grace. I was completely reliant on Him.

What a difficult time this was. I wasn't home with my other three children. They had to endure not only the absence of their mom for two months, but the delayed anticipation of meeting the baby brother they had prayed for. It was a very stressful time for my entire family. My husband was my rock. My church family filled in every gap for my family so I could be at the hospital.

I thought my fourth delivery would be like my other three—easy. Pop them out and away we go, rushing to get back into life. "Not this time," God said. *I came to realize that I had taken life for granted.* We expect the easiest way, wanting to avoid anything that interrupts our natural flow. Au contraire!

In the midst of this, I tried sharing my experience with some friends, hoping they could offer some needed advice. No one was able to help me navigate how my spiritual and physical worlds were shifting because they couldn't understand what I was experiencing. I saw, heard, and sensed what God was doing, but I really needed to process this experience out loud. The Lord was the only one who could understand and help me through this.

I was exhausted every day from no sleep the night before. I called the hospital every four hours to check on my baby boy. I hated to leave him. I needed to know how to pray constantly. I pressed into God more than I ever had for his little life. (Pressing in is to position yourself in a place of stillness so you can hear God.)

When we were finally released after 60 days, I almost felt like I was walking out of a prison. At home, I began adjusting to life with my fourth child and his special needs and integrating my other three children to our new life. Little did I know more change was coming.

When we took our son for his first preemie visit, the doctor said it was necessary to isolate him from crowds of people. At his recommendation, we spent two full years quarantined at home in order to give his lungs and immune system time to grow stronger. In this season, which I have come to call my "wilderness," God did an overhaul on me. I think back and laugh. I am a tough cookie! Sixty days was not going to give God enough time to make the necessary changes in me. He needed 730 of them, oy vey! Can I tell you something? At first, I hated it because I was removed from everything I enjoyed doing. However, once I started to hear the Holy Spirit and understand what He wanted to do, I actually started to enjoy the process.

Do you recall that God appointed a season for both Moses and the apostle Paul to be set apart for the purpose of transformation? I feel as though I can relate to them in some ways. *I believe rest either comes naturally because we obey God's voice, or because we are forced through our circumstances.* The apostle Paul was shipwrecked and imprisoned for years at a time. God used that time to speak to him and to prepare, train, and equip him for his next assignment. I get it. I lived it! I believe I'm still learning it. Can you relate to a time in your life that God may have slowed you down a bit? Did you ever consider that God might be in it?

Remember, for years before the premature delivery of my son, life had been a roller coaster of stress and extreme busyness. I had been busy doing so much outside my home in serving the church, running ministries, taking care of problems, etc. I didn't realize how my busyness was impacting my children. I wasn't taking the time to sit still. I wanted to do more for God, rather than just *be* with Him. In other words, *I was seeking performance over relationship.* **I got caught in the spiritual trap of doing.** I didn't know the difference.

The first six months home with my baby boy were sheer bliss. I was completely smitten with my precious little guy. I never once lacked the joy to give him the special care he required. I did, however, start to wonder why God removed me from all of my "jobs." I'll be completely honest—I struggled. I dug my heels in. I didn't like missing out on church and the areas I was responsible for. My mind ran wild, wondering why I was removed from life as I once knew it.

During that time period, the Lord held back many relationships. Of course, I didn't understand this at the time. I felt rejected. I was confused, upset, and overwhelmed with this shift in my relationships. God finally spoke to me, as clear as day. He told me I was right where He wanted me, and His was the only voice I was to listen to.

I had to learn God's voice. I had to be tuned in constantly to hear Him over my own voice and the voice of the enemy trying to derail me from the Lord's plan. He encouraged me that He would take care of all of my needs. And He did. Looking back, I still don't understand why the shift in my relationships remains, but I do know this: it was God's hand that held back those relationships for my good, so that He could do a work in me.

During this time I was very intentional to keep Sundays and Wednesdays for the Lord. I would watch several TV sermons, read, study, and pray. I was dedicated to maintaining my time with God. I loved Jesus so much! He was teaching me the "more" I was longing for. God was closer than ever. He didn't feel so far away.

Shortly into this hard wilderness of being home with my baby boy, away from life as I once knew it, The Lord put a book in my hands—*The Practice of the Presence of God* by Brother Lawrence. This book, written in the 1600s, challenged me to test myself on how much I kept God on my mind. Here is an excerpt from his summary:

> This collection of conversations and letters of Brother Lawrence, born Nicholas Herman, describe his daily habits in developing his relationship with an almighty being, God. Lawrence describes his spiritual journey from the time of his conversion, at eighteen, to just days before his death. He admonishes any person interested in an authentic religious experience to seek God continuously. If one does this, one attains a consistent

relationship with God. Attitudes such as selfless love and attention to detail evidence such a relationship.

Brother Lawrence sees God as his father, his friend, his judge, and his king, among other things. Each of these personifications of God arises at different points of Lawrence's life and spiritual journey. Contrary to spiritual advisors of his time, Lawrence advises devotees to seek God continually and simply, not using repetitive prayers at assigned times only. Secular activities sometimes distract one from one's desired devotion, but years of constant applications and confessions eventually bring one to a place of living in the presence of God.[2]

Well, I thought to myself, "I think of God all day long!" So, I set a day to test myself. I started my day at 9:00 a.m. thinking about Him and praising Him as I began my daily routine. When 5:00 p.m. came, I gasped in astonishment. I was all in during the first fifteen minutes, but had neglected to include Him in the rest of my day! My mind had been so full of garbage and nonsense and everything in between. I sobbed. I was disappointed to discover how little time and energy I spent actually thinking about God outside of my service to Him. The Holy Spirit was revealing the state I was in. I was in trouble.

I realized I had been independent when I should have been solely dependent on God. Most of us probably think we can handle all the little things on our own and just rely on God for the big things. *I needed to renew my mind. All this time, I had been thinking busyness was what I needed. But in reality, the busyness was a spiritual trap that kept me from what I wanted most—being in God's presence.*

In order to give me my heart's desire, God had to put me in a wilderness season. Having a premature child and spending two months in the hospital taught me to rely on God for *all* of my needs. Overwhelmed

---

[2] Lawrence, and John J. Delaney. 1977. *The practice of the presence of God.* New York: Image Books/Doubleday.

with the love of God, I gladly complied from that point forward. What a mindset shift!

The Lord put me in a holding pattern, so to speak. Being homebound for two years forced me to slow down, rest, and decompress. I was able to catch my breath for the first time in years. *I learned that being still had value and created intimacy between me and my Heavenly Father.* Staying in removed me from my busy lifestyle and allowed me to spend exorbitant amounts of time with Him. That's when I began unwrapping the great gift that is *the secret.* This was the ride of my life! My wilderness experience. This is why I can relate to Moses. I too was removed to be retrained, to unlearn life as I once knew it, and to be prepared for God to send me out fresh—mentally and spiritually fixed on Him. *I began practicing His presence.*

I pray that this personal, practical, biblical guide will be a tool to encourage you, inspire you, and lead you closer to the Trinity: Father, Son, and Holy Spirit. We need all three. They each have functions in our lives; it's vital to understand that.

> *And He said, "My presence shall go with*
> *you, and I will give you rest."*
>
> *Exodus 33:14*

CHAPTER 2

DISCOVERING THE SECRET

Follow me, track with me, as I take you on my journey of how I discovered the secret. It happened in stages. In and of themselves, the stages are significant. Packaged together, these stages, outlined in James 4:7-8, are powerful biblical principles that will transform your relationship with God.

Do you understand the power of the Gospel? That is the beginning of the secret.

The Gospel

While being transformed during my two years in the wilderness, one of the many things I pondered on was the power of the Gospel. The Gospel is the death, burial, and resurrection of Jesus Christ, and his appearance to the multitudes afterwards. It's simple in its simplicity. Oh, how much love He has for you and me. It's overwhelming! **The Gospel is the core of where we live from.** The Christian belief system rests on these truths. Understanding the magnitude of what Christ did for us, where He went, and what He delivered us, from compels us to live for Him. 1 Corinthians 15:1-7 clarifies this truth.

Living life from the power of the Gospel is the shift most of us desire to experience. Are you living *from* this power or living *towards* it? Understanding this principle changes everything. "That I may know Him, and the power of His resurrection, and the fellowship of His sufferings, being conformed to His death, in order that I may attain to the resurrection from the dead." Philippians 3:10,11

The Shift

When we come to Christ, we come with a level of awareness of what we know up to that point. Watching others helps us understand how to connect the dots. We begin to see the power of the Scriptures and how the Bible affects our lives as we try to apply it. Living towards the power, for me, was wanting more. I wanted what I saw in others and wanted more of what I read, but didn't yet understand how to obtain it.

I was stuck and kept getting in my own way. Until one day, the level of my understanding shifted off of myself, onto Jesus and the power of the Holy Spirit. It was a life-changing 'aha' moment that transformed the way I live. I no longer live *towards* the truth of the Gospel trying to get it to stick. I now live *from* the Gospel. I live with a mindset shift that it doesn't end with the Gospel, it begins with it.

The value of the meaning of the Gospel literally shaped my worldview, gave me new perspective on how I will react or respond to circumstances, and transformed my attitude from *me* to *He*. I live from the truth that Jesus paid a great price for my freedom and eternal life.

Everything has a cause and effect. When I embraced this truth, my motives shifted from selfish to Christ-centered. It's no longer about me, it's all about *Him*. Surrendering and aligning myself with His truth has given me boldness and courage to live from a place of Christ's authority in me. In and of myself, I have nothing. With Christ, I have everything.

We don't know what we don't know until we know it. Such an interesting statement, but think about it. It's true. We feel God is so far away from us, when in reality, we are the ones who are far from Him. We think we know so much, then we turn a corner in our growth and personal development. That's when we realize we really didn't know so much after all. We should never live with a closed mind, set in our particular ways. There is so much in this world that we have yet to learn that will add value to our growth. An open mind will grow our faith.

Pause: Consider this great truth—The power of the Gospel is life-changing. When we take in this truth, it will change our thinking and grow our understanding that life is just not about us. It's all about us, but at the same time, it's not about us. It's about what we do with it.

The Trinity

Do we understand who God, or the Trinity, really is? God, who is Lord of all, consists of the Father, Jesus the Son, and Holy Spirit. They have the same essence of deity. Although they work in unison, they have separate functions.

The Father—Sovereign and Creator of All

May I introduce to you the Creator of the universe! His name is God and here are just a few of His attributes. He is a supernatural being of holiness, righteousness, and power. He lives without limits! He has no beginning or end. He sees all, knows all, and has the power to do whatever He pleases. His power is displayed in His creation. He spoke the worlds into existence. He does not change, He cannot lie, He has absolute authority, and He is completely in control.

Jesus the Son—the Image of the Invisible God

Jesus came to earth as 100% God in 100% human form to reconcile the Father to His creation—human beings. Me and you. He is our salvation, the propitiation for our sins, our Redeemer, our Shepherd, and the Lamb of God. He is the Word of God in print and the Living Word in the flesh. He came as our friend and has made us His bride. *Jesus is the example of being a living sacrifice.* He validates the Father and is a reflection of His glory. God created all things through Jesus. The power of His resurrection has been passed on to His believers.

Holy Spirit—our Helper and Comforter.

The Holy Spirit was present at creation. He moved over the waters. The Holy Spirit is promised to those who confess Jesus Christ as their Lord and Savior. He is our gift. *He seals, empowers, convicts, protects, and guides us. He distributes spiritual gifts as He wills. As we abide in Him, He anoints us and teaches us all things in order to train us and prepare us for the Bridegroom.*

Three in One **describes the Trinity—***Inseparable, yet each individually important for our journey with God.* How do you see each Person of the triune God? Contemplate the importance of each and the role they have in your life.

Are you ready for more of the secret to unfold? The next principle is found in Psalm 46:10.

"Be still, and know that I am God."

To know that He is God . . . When I repeat that to myself, I immediately respond in my mind, ". . . and I am not!" How often do we try to play the role of God in our lives? Learning to trust and submit to His authority will help us to be still.

God exhorts us, "Know that I Am God." The "I Am" means to eternally exist. There are many scriptural references to God as the one true God. "Hear, O Israel! The LORD is our God, the LORD is one!" (Deuteronomy 6:4); "I am the LORD, and there is no other; Besides Me there is no God." (Isaiah 45:5). Once we begin to know Him, our desire to be still in His presence will continually grow.

Discovering the secret in stages is like the unveiling of the Trinity. It begins with the power of the Gospel and continues with the revelation of the functions of the Trinity, being still and knowing that He is God.

In being still and desiring to know God more, I contemplated the depth of the Gospel; I became much more aware of who God was and how much I needed Him. I was learning what was and was not important to God. My mindset shifted—I was starting to see that what I had deemed important was not so important after all. I was discovering the importance of greater things. He was answering my prayer.

The more I sought God, the more of the secret He revealed. To think it came through the premature birth of my son. He captured me and placed me under house arrest, like the apostle Paul. That's when He started pruning me, reshaping me, and helping me learn the truth I was missing. My mind was beginning to calm down, my heart was finding peace, and my body was at rest for the first time ever. The cherry on top was a beautiful baby boy in need of his momma's unconditional love.

Looking back, my wilderness season was one of the best times of my life. I had come to understand what intimacy with God looked like. *It is just being authentic and personal.* He was revealing His desire to be with me. He was helping me see my misunderstanding that doing more would help me find the satisfaction and fulfillment I was searching for.

He is jealous for me! He draws me to Himself to spend time with me. I was too busy to see or understand that. My head was full of so many unnecessary random thoughts, I couldn't hear His voice. I was not maintaining a healthy relationship with Him, period. Notice, we had a relationship. I was a believer; I loved Him. But because I was not in communion with Him, I was caught in a spiritual trap that poisoned my contribution to our relationship.

Have you ever contemplated what it really means to have communion with God? To walk with God and do daily life with Him? Communing is talking together intimately; being in close spiritual harmony (with).[3] It's practicing His presence.

In the Scriptures, 1 Corinthians 11:17-34 tells of the Lord's Supper. Jesus communed with His disciples. He was intimate and spent quality time with them. He loved them, taught them, and spoke of things to come. On the night He was betrayed, they took communion together in His honor. He was among them, not a far distant God.

In the two years I spent home with my son, communion became an intricate part of my relationship with Jesus. It was not to be rushed

---

[3] Webster's New World College Dictionary, 4th Edition. Copyright © 2010 by Houghton Mifflin Harcourt. All rights reserved.

or taken lightly. I spent time examining myself in light of the Gospel. I was intentional to confess my sins daily. By being aware of myself, I was able to submit myself to His authority on a daily basis. Concentrating on the cross and His presence was like stepping out of the darkness and living completely exposed in the light.

How many of us want a relationship with God, yet spend more time serving Him than we do spending time with Him? I have asked many people that I counsel and coach how much time they spend communing with God. Many respond that they're just too busy, but they give as much time as they can to serve. They misunderstand, thinking this is the sum of their relationship with God. I'm sure this is not what God had in mind when He created us to do life with Him. Many of us just don't realize how we get trapped in the busyness of life. If I asked you, "How much time do you spend alone with God?" What would your answer be?

God desires an intimate relationship with you. In your experience, what does it take to build a healthy relationship? Do you spend a lot of time with the other person? Do you come up with intimate opportunities to surprise them? Do you enjoy heart-to-heart conversations? What would it do to our relationships if we weren't intentional to do those things?

Pause: Do we understand the difference between serving the Creator and having an intimate relationship with Him?

There are many traps that can take us captive. Through my personal experience, I hope to bring truth and understanding, and help you identify the spiritual traps in your life so you can be set free.

The Lord has activated these biblical principles in my life, empowered me, and awakened me to the secret of a closer walk with God. I'm so excited about how much the Lord loves me, little old me! I'm passionate and head over heels in love with Him. He is so faithful. *Not only is He a good God, He is good to us and He is good for us.* Can you tell by my excitement, I love to learn and grow? God is the treasure I love to dig for!

Jesus is my hero, my mentor, my beloved. He has enlightened me and given me a deeper awareness of who He is in my life. I've experienced much in my years with the Lord. I've learned a lot through many trials and disappointments. I've been pruned and molded, and am still in the process of being perfected. I have seen the power and glory of God come through in miracles and in answers to prayer and fasting.

I was prompted to share my story because the majority of those that I teach, mentor, disciple, coach, and counsel ask me repeatedly, "Why haven't I learned this?" I think it's time to bring awareness to one special exhortation that God gives all of us as believers in the Body of Christ. It will change your life. It changed mine! I find that many are not being encouraged or mentored in this one area. It is rarely mentioned.

A common response to this concept has been, "That's evil!" or "Oh no, I would never!" among others. I'm left dumbfounded. It's in the Bible! I'm shocked that so many people reject this practice. I believe this is yet another spiritual trap meant to keep us from drawing closer to the God we long for.

Here it is—the unveiling! The principle that so few people are putting into practice is . . . **biblical meditation,** or being still with God.[4] Let's press in, asking God to shift our mindsets and show us the difference between our understanding of meditation and what biblical meditation really is.

Psalm 1:2 says, "But his delight is in the law of the Lord, and in His law he meditates day and night." I would like to offer a prayer for us before I go any further.

> Father, in Jesus' name, we bring this chapter to you. Help us understand what meditation is. Father, we want to hear from You. We desire You to guide us and teach us. Moreover, help us understand how You have designed meditation for our benefit and that applying Your principles will keep us from spiritual traps. I ask, Lord, that You anoint these words. I pray they bless the

---

[4] Psalm 46:10, Psalm 119:15, 16

reader, and I pray, Father, that they inspire and motivate us to action. All for Your glory and intimacy with Your people. May we all draw closer under Your wing. In Jesus' name, Amen.

I need you to understand something from the get-go. Biblical meditation is not a spiritual trap! Lack of meditation is what entangles you in a spiritual trap.

Being still is to let down, or cease from, frantic activity. Meditation is "giving your attention to only one thing; serious thought or study."[5] There are many words we can use interchangeably with meditation: being still, sitting quietly, pondering, being intentional to think deeply on something, relaxing, decompressing, seeking God's presence and peace, pressing in, soaking, being filled and seeking more, quieting your soul, and waiting on the Lord.

The Lord positioned me in a posture of being still by ceasing my frantic activity during my time in the wilderness.

Meditation is an opportunity to steady your mind and heart on the things of the Lord—His Word, His Holiness, His greatness, His righteousness, and your need for Him—so you can hear His voice. It slows you down, calms you, and centers your soul in His peaceful presence. It causes you to focus on His ways, rather than your own. Meditation enables you to truly connect with God, who is the source of all we need. It requires being intentional in order to remove noise pollution and outside distractions. It is so simple, yet painstakingly hard for most of us. It requires us to flip our mindsets.

Pause: Do you use the word **meditation**? Do you practice meditating? Do you know what the Bible says about it?

Jeremiah 29:13 (paraphrase) says, "seek Me and you will find Me." Jesus invited us to meditate when He said to "go into your closet and shut the door." (Matthew 6:6 KJV paraphrase) He demonstrated the

---

[5] "Meditation." Cambridge Dictionary, dictionary.cambridge.org/us/dictionary/english/meditation.

17

importance of meditation and was our example when He went away from the crowds to be alone with the Father.[6]

Biblical meditation is for born again believers who have trusted Jesus Christ as their Lord and Savior and desire to draw closer to Him. It is for the purpose of developing a relationship with Jesus and applying His principles. It's that simple. A lack of desire to meditate is a spiritual trap. Why, you may ask? Because it keeps you from a deeper relationship with Jesus. How will we get to know Jesus more if we are never intentional about setting time aside to spend with Him? This is where meditation, or being still, comes into play.

Are you being encouraged to meditate? Does anyone hold you accountable to practice meditation? We need people to encourage us to draw closer to God. I hope the tools I put in your hand will be the encouragement you need.

Our Enemy

Consider this: *We need to know who our enemy is and how he sets his traps.* This is very important for us to understand. Genesis chapter 1 says God created everything and said it was good. Stated briefly, Satan the fallen angel, enemy of God, full of pride, kicked out of heaven . . . comes prancing along. He is our enemy. He is the accuser of the brethren. He counterfeits the good and twists the truth just enough to set us up for failure. Just observe his tactics in Genesis chapter 3. Satan set a trap. He subtly led Eve into disobedience to God. In John 10:10, Jesus calls him a thief who comes only to steal, kill, and destroy.

Our adversary, Satan, would prefer us to fail at everything, especially our relationship with our Heavenly Father. He plots to disconnect our minds from seeking after God, knowing God, or desiring to follow after God. He tries to lure us into a position that makes us feel far away from God. *The enemy is not lazy. He is cunning and divisive.* He works overtime to confuse God's people and keep them busy. Very busy. If he can distract us enough, we can miss one of the greatest benefits of our Christian walk. If he can create chaos and keep us busy to the point

---

[6] Matthew 14:23, Luke 6:12

that we don't get an opportunity to be with Jesus to read, learn, and memorize His Word, we lose. Intimacy comes from communing alone in a quiet place with the Lord.

Spiritual Traps and Distractions—an Epidemic!

Spiritual traps draw you away from God. We must learn to identify them and be set free. I ask again, what keeps *you* from drawing closer to God? Why does God feel so far away? When we're entrapped, it is so easy to go astray. As a result, we can create our own ideas about what a relationship with God should look like. Many, like I did, are missing the mark. Many people try to control their own outcome. This breaks my heart. A healthy biblical lifestyle is dependent upon these powerful principles, yet the Body of Christ has been neglecting their application. I see this as an epidemic.

Many people avoid meditation altogether because they don't understand what it is or maybe they've been told it is New Age. Yep! You guessed it, another spiritual trap. Satan tries to counterfeit God's practice for drawing closer to Him. When he succeeds, he keeps most believers from experiencing a deeper, closer walk with God.

Basic Christianity is really about surrendering your life to the Lord Jesus Christ and seeking and following after Him. Being a follower of Christ takes intentional time getting to know the One we are following. Psalm 46:10 says, "Be still, and know that I am God." Jesus works in and through us to do things that in and of ourselves, we would never be able to do. God, the Creator of all good things, is the source of all we need. Let's face it. If you haven't put meditation into practice, you don't know what you're missing out on.

If the enemy can keep you from doing something that benefits you, he wins. He truly wins. Let's get our heads in the game. I encourage you to have a competitive heart for spiritual things. Be at the top of your game to ensure the enemy loses. We must be girded with biblical truth so he doesn't get an advantage on us. We should always be two steps ahead of him.

Remember that the fruit of the Spirit is love, joy, peace, patience, kindness, goodness, faithfulness, gentleness, self-control; against such things there is no law.[7] If we are not experiencing these, something is out of balance. Of course we will be stressed and overwhelmed if we're so busy that we don't take time out with God. This is exactly why God wants us to rest and be still. There will be evidence of good fruit in those who are in the spirit, as opposed to those who are not.

Socrates said, "Beware the barrenness of a busy life." Satan's primary weapon of busyness entraps us with stress, anxiety, and worry, just to name a few. If we're not careful, they can grow into depression, loneliness, and isolation. As we learn to identify those traps, we can begin to tear them down. *Meditating on God's truth enables us to reel in wayward thoughts and regain a right focus.* Scripture says in 2 Corinthians 10:5, "Casting down imaginations, and every high thing that exalteth itself against the knowledge of God, and bringing into captivity every thought to the obedience of Christ;" (KJV). We should not dwell on negative, unlovely, or condemning thoughts; they are not of God. It's spiritual warfare!

There is so much to take in—the benefits of meditation, some consequences that come with lack of meditation, and what proactively meditating might look like. I hope this helps you see that we can't afford not to meditate.

Meditation is not an option, it's a necessity!

I have personally experienced how vital meditation is. God knew that in our busy lives we would need to find our balance in Him. Meditation is an intimate time to connect and bond with our Creator.

We live in a busy, busy world. Can you see how we might feel as though God is so far away? The times we live in are busier than probably any other generation before us. There are a lot of distractions, good and bad. Distractions are spiritual traps that keep us too busy to spend time with God. The question is, will we slow down and eliminate what hinders us from taking the time to be with God?

---

[7] Galatians 5:22, 23

The enemy's mission is to keep you from your God. Is he succeeding?

Again, the lack of biblical mediation is a spiritual trap. I hope to help you understand what biblical meditation really is and how necessary it is for your life. We don't want to miss out on this principle that God has given us. We really don't. He designed this time for multiple blessings for us and Himself. It's our lifeline. It's so beneficial. It's essential for us to meditate and practice being in His presence.

This truly was the Lord's design to benefit us and bless Him in our time of communing. It starts and ends with the Word of God, pressing in to be with Jesus and being centered on Him. It's not emptying your mind or being mindless. Our techniques focus on Father, Son, and Holy Spirit.

All religious meditation is not the same. For example, the meditative practices associated with the religion and philosophy of Buddhism encompass a variety of meditation techniques that aim to develop mindfulness, concentration, supramundane powers, tranquility, and insight.[8] Every religion bases their own meditation practices around their beliefs and connection to their superior being.

It is imperative for the Body of Christ to recognize that biblical meditation is not a philosophy—it is an exhortation for us to slow down from our busy lives in order to have a closer walk with our Creator.

My life's calling is to empower the Body of Christ to reach its fullest potential and to live the abundant life in Christ. In over twenty-five years of counseling and coaching, I've seen many principles being left out. All I can say is, it's never too late!

God invites us to participate in meditation with Him.

I hope that you take advantage of opportunities to come to know Jesus more personally. Here is what our offering to the Lord might look like:

---

[8] https://en.m.wikipedia.org/wiki/Buddhist_meditation

"Let the words of my mouth and the meditation of my heart be acceptable in Your sight, O LORD, my rock and my Redeemer." (Psalm 19:14)

"Let my meditation be pleasing to Him; As for me, I shall be glad in the LORD." (Psalm 104:34)

The Lord enjoys our meditation. When we take time out of our busy schedules and ponder on Him, it pleases Him. When we are in obedience, it will bring great joy to us and God. Oh come, let us adore Him! Oh, may our hearts be acceptable in His sight, who is our Rock and Redeemer. May our meditation be pleasing to Him. What pleases God? That we seek Him by faith, walk in the Spirit and not in the flesh, and walk worthy of our calling. We are able to do these things by the power of His Spirit who lives within us.

My meditation practices developed over time as I was in my wilderness. Desiring more of God in my life, I set time aside to press in. Why do I need more of God? Because I'm wretched. I'm empty. I need transformation. I truly want to reflect His glory and bring Him honor. Another reason is that my days can be hectic. I might be stressed, tired, and feeling empty from pouring myself out for others all day. I go to my secret place to be still, ponder on His holiness and righteousness, or meditate on a verse. This is what I need to relax and center my thoughts on God. Meditation brings clarity and a pure perspective.

The Holy Spirit led me to teach an entire women's weekend retreat around this topic. God highly values meditation. The *Be Still and Know that I am God* Revival was built on learning that exact statement taken right out of the book of Psalms. We devoted an entire afternoon to being still. The *Meditation Stations* workshops are included in the last chapter of this book. I share this so you can see what many women experienced and discovered during their very first time of intentionally being still with the Lord. The results were overwhelmingly amazing! I hope after spending this time with me, you will consider planning your own personal retreat with God.

How deep are you willing to go with God? Can I ask you to have an open mind and an open heart to receive?

Here is what we should be asking ourselves: Why don't I press in? What am I missing out on? What do I miss out on when I don't? What are the consequences of not pressing in? This brings us back to why many believers may seem to avoid meditation. It just may be they are uncomfortable with meditation; if so, that doesn't mean it's wrong. It may mean God wants to stretch you. He definitely wants to get alone with you and help you decompress from a busy life. We should be like the Bereans, studying every day so that we can make biblical, educated decisions from sound, factual information out of the Scriptures. Don't you agree?

It really boils down to this: we need to ask ourselves, *What does God require of me?* Micah 6:8 gives us a little insight. "He has told you, O man, what is good; And what does the LORD require of you, but to do justice, to love kindness, and to walk humbly with your God?" Meditation will lead us into more humility. As we seek Him, we will become more like Him. As we find Him, we will discover He is the essence of humility.

Are you excited? Are you ready to dive in and get an idea of how beneficial meditation can be for your life? I hope you will be encouraged to apply this biblical concept. After all, it may be the secret to living the life you've been searching for. Applying these suggestions is a great place to start! I encourage you to sit still and to know your God more intimately. Do you know how much God loves you? He loves you so much and is delighted to spend time with you. He is waiting with open arms. What's holding you back? Let's dive in!

Want to put some time aside for the Lord right now? Let's give it a try. I'll walk you through it. Here are a few verses that motivated me to press in and really ponder the importance of their meanings. You may even want to memorize them. Scripture memorization is a good way to meditate on God and His Word. We're going to read these verses two times, slowly and out loud. (Notice I've written the verses twice for that reason.) Really hear what you're saying. You're up, let's try this!

- "Be still, and know that I am God." (Psalm 46:10 KJV)
- "Be still, and Know that I am God."
- "Wait on the Lord; be of good courage, and He shall strengthen your heart. Wait, I say, on the Lord!" (Psalm 27:14 NKJV)
- "Wait on the Lord; be of good courage, and He shall strengthen your heart. Wait, I say, on the Lord!"
- "Rest in the LORD, and wait patiently for Him." (Psalm 37:7)
- "Rest in the LORD, and wait patiently for Him."
- "Surely I have calmed and quieted my soul, like a weaned child with his mother; like a weaned child is my soul within me." (Psalm 131:2 NKJV)
- "Surely I have calmed and quieted my soul, like a weaned child with his mother; like a weaned child is my soul within me."
- "Meditate in your heart upon your bed, and be still." (Psalm 4:4)
- "Meditate in your heart upon your bed, and be still."
- "He gives power to the weak, and to those who have no might He increases strength. Even the youths shall faint and be weary, and the young men shall utterly fall, but those who wait on the LORD shall renew their strength. They shall mount up with wings like eagles. They shall run and not be weary; they shall walk and not faint." (Isaiah 40:29-31 NKJV)
- "He gives power to the weak, and to those who have no might He increases strength. Even the youths shall faint and be weary, and the young men shall utterly fall, but those who wait on the LORD shall renew their strength. They shall mount up with wings like eagles. They shall run and not be weary; they shall walk and not faint."

Pause: Let's see what else there is to be found. Right now, set a timer for at least fifteen minutes. Be still and ask yourself questions by breaking down each verse. Ask God, "What significant meaning do these verses have for me?" If you'd like, write down what you hear or see.

Did you take time to really digest what the Word of God was saying to you? I hope you enjoyed that exercise. Did the Lord reveal anything new to you? Write down what He showed you.

> *So Jesus was saying to those Jews who had*
> *believed Him, "If you continue in My word,*
> *then you are truly disciples of Mine"*
>
> *John 8:31*

CHAPTER 3

RENEWING YOUR MIND

The alarm goes off! We jump out of bed, our feet hit the ground, and we mindlessly tackle our day, scrambling to fulfill our commitments. The last thing we need is unwanted interruptions like forgotten lunches or flat tires. Our schedules are overbooked and we are overwhelmed with responsibilities.

We run ourselves ragged all day, only to come home to even more busyness of meals, laundry, chores, errands, and such. We never seem to decompress. Is it any wonder we crash into bed each night, exhausted?

Can you relate? When you hit the bed, you're restless. Does your mind race with all the unfinished business that awaits you tomorrow? Do details keep you up at night? Or maybe you're the type that passes out as soon as you hit the bed—until that dreaded moment, somewhere in your REM sleep, you feel the pressure against your bladder. You tell yourself, "don't get up, don't get up . . . oh no, I have to get up!" You walk yourself to the bathroom, trying to stay asleep, not opening your eyes, feeling your way through the dark because you know as soon as your mind becomes conscious, it will start racing again. Your mind takes over as soon as you get back to bed; you stare at the ceiling, wishing you were able to sleep, wanting to turn your mind off—but it just won't stop.

We have our minds so wound up with details and busyness that they never want to shut off. Yes, another spiritual trap. We race through our days like zombies. Maybe there's so much talk of the zombie apocalypse because we are all running around on autopilot, dragging with exhaustion, looking pretty dead. Don't you agree that most of us are running the rat race?

This describes so many women I've counseled over the years. Is this you? It was me. It . . . *was* . . . me. Did you see that? It was me—past tense—a long time ago. I may not be able to help you with your overactive bladder, but all joking aside, I can help you free yourself from an overactive mind that runs your life.

Have you ever wished you could just get a good night's sleep? Do you struggle with negative emotions, experience brain fog, or lack clarity of thoughts? We give free space to unwanted tenants! I'd like to introduce the idea of renewing your mind. What does that mean? It means replacing the old with the new. It means purging the clutter of negative thoughts. Slowing down our racing minds brings us to a place of peace and calm.

For me, it also meant deprogramming from autopilot reactions and coming to a true understanding of why I do what I do. **One of the most important transformational moments in my life was when I took control of my thought life and took responsibility to renew my mind continually, according to the Scriptures.**

This was no overnight success story. I had to be honest with myself. I had to have the courage to conqueror my fears. I had to wrestle with negative thoughts that told me I wasn't good enough, remember when, you're not loved. . . blah, blah, blah. You know the constant condemning thoughts that work against you. This spiritual trap kept me paralyzed in my own head.

Renewing your mind is a lifestyle. I learned that if I read over God's promises until I believed them and trusted in how much He loved me, I was able to replace negative thoughts with His truth. We must be proactive to practice this daily. "Casting down imaginations, and every high thing that exalteth itself against the knowledge of God, and bringing into captivity every thought to the obedience of Christ:" (2 Corinthians 10:5 KJV) We must be intentional watchmen over our minds.

Isn't it crazy how many thoughts come up against us throughout the day? One day, a year or two after I became a believer, I was vacuuming, minding my own business, enjoying my day. All of a sudden, I became annoyed and angry without any interactions with anyone else. This was the first time I had ever recognized such a shift. I started asking myself why I was so mad. The enemy had sent in thoughts that were both false and evil. This created an internal turmoil, or torment, in my mind. I was full of frustration and the scenario hadn't even happened. Can you relate to this?

This was yet another spiritual trap. It keeps you so caught up in your own mind, focused on things that are not real. I call this spiritual trap "Satan's playpen." Once he lures you into an unhealthy thought, you engage in his play, and he's got you there all day! I had to learn to counteract with the Holy Word of God. From that day forward I have worked on being intentional to identify what I am disturbed about, the source of the disturbance, and how the Lord desires me to deal with it.

This is a common struggle experienced by the women I counsel. Here's a familiar scenario: You say hello to someone, or maybe you make eye contact and smile, expecting them to return the acknowledgment. Instead, they don't acknowledge you. They may even give you an un-kind look. The first thought that hits you is, "Did I do something to offend them? I can't believe they just ignored me." This can vex you. How long do you spend wondering whether they have a problem with you—an hour? a day? a week? a month? All the while, the enemy fuels you with divisive thoughts, such as "Boy, they're rude . . . what kind of friend are they . . . what's their problem?" along with any false accu-sations against them. Thus being caught in the playpen of our minds!

If we learn to stop that negative thought, tear it down and replace it with the benefit of the doubt, such as, "maybe they didn't see me, or they're distracted, thinking about other things," we will be much better off. We are followers of Christ in training. When we are offended so eas-ily that we take things personally without facts, we are bound in chains to the unhealthy thoughts and emotions that keep us in the playpen.

Can you see how meditation may be difficult when our minds are consumed with offenses? In our personal disgruntlement, we can easily justify our own sin. We blame our emotional baggage on those who we feel caused it, never seeing our part in being lured into the playpen of our minds. The other party has no idea we're struggling or upset with them. We protect ourselves from what we assume are hurtful offenses. Most of the time they are not even true! As followers of Jesus, we must put on the mind of Christ. *Counteracting with scripture can look like this: Great peace have they who love thy law and nothing shall offend them. (Psalm 119:165)*

Years ago, I counseled a woman who struggled over thoughts that her husband was cheating on her. We spent a lot of time combing through questions and answers that led her to this conclusion. She kept repeating that she didn't have proof, she just knew. Hmmm. How did she "just know?" I asked for evidence to understand how she thought she was right to "just know." We kept coming up empty.

She had convinced herself this was the truth and her emotions were sold out to it, yet there was no evidence. Finally, the Holy Spirit prompted me to ask, "What do you watch on television?" This is when we got to the bottom of her suspicions. It was soap operas! I asked about the storyline she was following. You guessed it. Adultery, affairs, rejection, and betrayal—all sin and fears of *what if*. She was caught in the spiritual trap of *What If.* She had to admit her fears came from a show that was playing on her emotions. She had zero facts!

Our minds can be stuck on thoughts that are not even real. *Left unchecked, our minds are notorious for setting us up for failure.* We allow our minds to play out *what if* scenarios when we are caught in this spiritual trap. Consequently, we waste lots of time conjuring up our own false reality. We can inadvertently be stuck on a thought that has us going in the wrong direction for years. We should not give so much mental space to destructive thoughts.

This is just one more way the enemy captures our minds and uses it against us. It can be so damaging. This woman's poor husband had no idea what he was up against! By the way, I asked how much time she spent meditating in the Word. She wasn't. She was too busy! She was overwhelmed, her mind out of control believing a lie, and she lived in fear based on what she thought her husband was doing. It paralyzed her and kept her from seeking God.

God can feel far away because of our sin. *Counteracting with scripture can look like this: For God has not given us the spirit of fear; but of power, and of love, and of a sound mind. (2 Timothy 1:7)*

This happens to more of us than we care to admit. We must be intentional to break the cycle. What we put in is what will come out. If I fill a bucket with garbage, garbage comes out when I empty it. If I fill a bucket with gold, gold will come out. If we fill our minds with Jesus, Scripture, and worship, guess what will come out? We must pay attention to what we feed our minds with. It's time to put the trash out once and for all.

If you're a visual learner, try this exercise: Close your eyes. In your mind's eye, try visualizing yourself sorting through all of your thoughts. Separate the negative from the positive. Take those negative thoughts that are cluttering your mind and stuff them into garbage bags. Carry them to the curb and place them where the trash truck would pick them up. Now, visualize walking back to the house. As you reach the door, turn around and look. The garbage truck is coming. Do you hear it? It stops to pick up all of your mess. As it drives away, wave bye-bye, breathe a sigh of relief, and realize you are not picking it back up. It is off to the dump where it belongs. Then make a commitment to be aware of what you allow into your thought life.

Allowing our minds to be lured into Satan's playpen is sin. When we oppose God and counteract His ways, we need to take responsibility to acknowledge our sin and submit ourselves to His authority. We can judge our behavior by the fruit we display. Is it the fruit of the Spirit or flesh? Sometimes we need to just get out of His way, trust Him for the outcome, and most of all, be willing vessels to confess and repent from our sin. He is faithful and just to forgive us.

Can I challenge your mindset right now? Let's read this together.

> "Therefore I urge you, brethren, by the mercies of God, to present your bodies a living and holy sacrifice, acceptable to God, which is your spiritual service of worship. And do not be conformed to this world, but be transformed by the renewing of your mind, so that you

may prove what the will of God is, that which is good
and acceptable and perfect." (Romans 12:1,2)

Let's break this down. Do not be conformed to this world. What
does that mean to you? Walk through this with me.

Pause: Take a moment to ponder this verse if you never have before. It's in your best interest to go deep with this. What does not being
conformed to this world mean to you?

What did you come up with? How have you been conformed to
the world, as opposed to how you've been transformed by the Word of
God? Does it look different?

Paul tells us not to be conformed to the world, but to be transformed. How does he want us to be transformed? He says, "by the
renewing of your mind." How do we renew our minds? They're so full
of clutter and lots of junk. It's been discovered that we have between
50,000-70,000 thoughts a day. Break that down to 35-48 thoughts
per minute. That's a lot of thoughts! We take things in from the news,
TV, movies, and media. We take in negative and positive emotions and
energy from people we work with, from our own personal hardships,
and maybe even from some traditions. How does this affect us? Have
you ever thought about it?

Our minds have been so bombarded with the filth and sin of the
world, we have become desensitized to it. We don't realize the trauma
we put ourselves through emotionally with what we allow to entertain
us. For instance, pornography has robbed and destroyed so many minds
and lives. This spiritual trap has taken them captive.

Is it any wonder Paul says, "Do not be conformed to this world,
but be transformed by the renewing of your mind?" Many of us have
an unhealthy, unstable mind. Many minds struggle with defeating
thoughts and condemning accusations. These spiritual traps keep us
from pressing in with Jesus and make us ineffective for the kingdom
of God. Do you see how the things we accept and conform to keep us
far from God?

Jesus gave His life to forgive us for *all* of our sins, including the ones we have been entrapped in. If the spiritual trap of pornography has overtaken you, confess, repent, turn from your sin, and press into His love and forgiveness. Be encouraged! There is nothing that God won't forgive you for. He loves you, He created you, and He has given you eternal life through Jesus if you believe.

Putting into practice the many suggestions here on renewing your mind will set you free and give you the ability to be at rest even in the middle of a hectic day. If you want to sleep better, YouTube has some lovely options to listen to. You might want to try listening to a harp playing hymn music or a narrator reading verses on peace. As you listen, take in the verses being poured over you; you are renewing your mind with God's truth. There is power in His Word! This is a biblical concept that even King David practiced. Psalm 63:6 says, "When I remember You on my bed, I meditate on You in the night watches." *Internal peace of mind will enable you to navigate through all of the negative forces that come up against you throughout the day.*

Remember I said that I seem to learn things the hard way? Well, my mind was like Speed Racer. At one point in my life, listening to my own voice, I think I spoke faster than I was even able to comprehend. I really wonder how people put up with me. I had no idea I was entangled in the spiritual trap of an overactive mind—until I was flat on my back with copper toxicity.

My entire internal system was off and it was manifesting itself in some unusual ways. The overload of copper in my body brought on chronic fatigue. I lay on the sofa, exhausted from nothingness. My mind had stopped functioning properly because I was intoxicated with metals. My mind went completely blank. I was shocked—I had no thoughts. Honestly, I would lay there thinking, "I have nothing to think about!"

At that time, the very thought of details or busyness exhausted me. I couldn't bear to think of all the things I had to do that I didn't have the energy for. This was a first for me. Where I once had multiple things on my mind, now I had nothing. Here is where I learned that my mind was not at rest. One of my most important takeaways from this experience was learning the value of having peace of mind. Once I recovered from copper toxicity, I made it a point to not entertain an overactive mind. *Counteracting with scripture can look like this: "Search me, O God, and know my heart; Try me and know my anxious thoughts." (Psalms 139:23)*

Pause: I encourage you to accept a mindset shift. It starts with being honest with yourself about where your mind is. Once I started on the path of shifting from what I *thought* I knew to what I *needed* to know, my world changed from the inside out.

Renewing your mind begins as you make wise choices on what you let into your mind. Then, find the appropriate Scripture verses to read, study, memorize and proclaim over yourself to flush out the garbage. *Transformation will come when you change your intake.* Soon those thoughts that once took you captive will no longer have power over you. You will defend yourself with God's Word and replace negative lies with positive truth. You will be equipped to understand how to escape the trap. It truly is a lifestyle change.

Believing what God says about you in Scripture also helps renew your mind. For example, Proverbs 23:7 tells us, "For as you think in your heart, so are you." (NKJV paraphrase) Challenge your thoughts and your thought process. Your mind can be tamed! What consumes your mind? Asking yourself this question will help you understand the way you think.

Renewing your mind by meditating on the Word of God will change how you think. It will start to declutter the junk. It exposes the lies that you have believed and lived out. It starts with reading and obeying the Scriptures, surrendering our wants, our desires, and our needs over to God in order to live out this life according to His Word. Remember the apostle Paul says that it's not only so you prove what is good, but also so you discover what is acceptable and the perfect will of God. As the Word transforms your mind, you will find what is acceptable and what is His perfect will. Meditation is so vital for mental clean up.

Don't be afraid to make these necessary changes. Fear grips all of us in one way or another. Yet another spiritual trap! 2 Timothy 1:7 assures us that God has not given us the spirit of fear, but of power, love, and a sound mind. By renewing our minds, we can overcome the fears that paralyze us and keep us from living the abundant life.

Are you ready to make healthy lifestyle changes? Together, we can conqueror this. The Lord tells us we are overcomers. Let us overcome!

Friend, we all struggle at times to keep God at the forefront. This is not a condemnation, it's an encouragement we could all benefit from. It's meant to inspire and cause you to desire to practice meditation. I use the word "practice" because really, whenever you put something into action and you do it over and over again, it's practice that makes a change in your lifestyle. If you are playing in a sporting event, you practice. You create an opportunity to go through movements and training to get things down right. It's a matter of setting time aside to step into training. Meditation is so beneficial; it's such a gift. Part of that gift is renewing your mind.

God has given us the perfect gift in Scripture to illustrate this principle. Psalm 23:1-3 (NKJV) says, "The Lord is my shepherd; I shall not want. He makes me to lie down in green pastures; He leads me beside the still waters. He restores my soul; He leads me in the paths of righteousness for His name's sake."

Think about sitting on a green plush bank at the edge of a stream or a brook that is flowing nicely, trickling against the rocks. This atmosphere is relaxing and soothing to the ear. It puts you in a posture to be still.

But here, the Lord says, "I want you to sit beside the still waters," and here's why. When we sit still long enough and we're relaxed, He can work on us. Notice this Scripture doesn't say that He leads you beside the rushing waters. Rushing waters create anxiety and stress. (Try it for yourself. Listen to a few YouTube videos. Compare the sound of rushing water to a gentle brook or stream.) Rushing water creates a sense of unease. The unexpected crashes of the river current would take you by surprise and build up anxiety. You could sit there for a while but you'd feel like it's time to get up and do something, because the constant sound of the rushing water creates movement.

God can't work on us when we're busy running around, b
our minds aren't set on Him. But when we take time out to po
ourselves to hear from Him, to renew our minds, the Holy Spirit
His work. He restores our soul and leads us in the path of righteousn
for His name's sake.

Meditation is so beneficial! Why aren't we obeying the Scriptures?
They are soooooo good for us! It took me so long to come to understand
this. I wasn't taught this. Many of us *just don't know.* Praise God for
His truth and the power of the Holy Spirit within us that teaches and
guides us into *all* truth. Press in, my friends. It is so worth it! Take time
to identify where your mind is. You will be glad you did.

Your investment in yourself will determine your return. Early
on in my walk with God, I realized He had His hands full with me. I
didn't give my life to Christ until I was 23 years old; I was self-absorbed.
I truly needed to understand myself, my thought process, and my heart
motive in everything I did.

The most important person to study outside of Jesus is yourself. It is
good to examine ourselves in order to identify our growth patterns.
Self-awareness equals God awareness. God created us and He resides
in us after we trust in Christ for salvation. Remember that! We should
be ever growing on a steady, consistent basis as we spend precious time
with the Lord. It should result in our desire to love Him more, to the
point we just can't get enough. This is a journey of growth.

Well, friends, are you excited to see how God can transform your
life when you renew your mind?

> *Thou wilt keep him in perfect peace, whose mind*
> *is stayed on Thee: because he trusteth in Thee.*
>
> Isaiah 26:3 KJV

CHAPTER 4

HEARING GOD

In the beginning of my journey with Jesus, I had to learn God's voice. I often struggled to hear from Him and obey what He asked me to do. Truthfully, it's because I spent more time talking to God than I spent listening. I ran ahead of Him because I hadn't yet learned the art of being still. I didn't understand what meditation was. I have come to discover God had always been speaking to me. I just had to learn how to recognize His voice over the other voices competing for my attention.

It was a bright sunny day in June when my husband and I decided to head to the beach for the day. We set up our umbrella in the spot we had been going to for over 25 years, situated our chairs facing the sun just right and ahhhhh, relaxation. As our beautiful day progressed, I needed to use the facilities. It was a long walk to get there.

As I walked along the beach, I passed two large groups of young folks. As I walked through the open space between them I sensed God nudging me, but wasn't quite sure what it was about. A young man passed me as I approached the bathhouse. God told me, "He will be in the group of people I want you to talk to." I asked, "What?" He said, "I want you to go over and tell the young lady in nursing school that she didn't make a mistake, it is exactly where I want her. Encourage her to stay the course." I put my fingers in my ears like a five-year-old and said, "La la la la la, I can't hear you! Lord, I don't want to walk over to a group of young kids and make a fool out of myself, really!" He responded, "You'll never know unless you go."

36

I started my journey back and as I came to the circle of twenty-some chairs, I leaned down near one of the girls. I said, "Hi. This may be the craziest thing that happens to you today. The Lord asked me to come over and talk with the young lady that is in nursing school." All eyes landed on the girl to my left. She looked at me with wide eyes. I was nervous and trembling inside as I asked her if she had contemplated dropping out of school, thinking she had made a mistake. She asked, "How do you know that?"

I said, "The Lord told me to come and tell you that you are right where you should be, that you did not make a mistake, and to stay the course. He is with you." She exclaimed, "Oh my gosh, I can't believe it!" I said, "Jesus loves you so much, He wants you to know it's all ok." Some of the other young people there asked, "Ooh, what about us?" I laughed and said, "This isn't fortune telling. This is a word from the God who created the universe. It doesn't work like that. It's what He has to say, when He wants to say it." They were all amazed. I shared how much God loves them all, then walked back to my chair.

Now my husband was watching the whole scene from afar, wondering what in the world I was doing. I giggled because he knows you never know where I may end up when the Lord starts talking. So I shared what just happened. I went to sit down and I was literally halfway to parking myself back in the sun when Holy Spirit said, "You need to go back." I thought, *What!* He continued, "They're hungry for Me. Go back." I said, "You stopped talking to me. What else was I supposed to say?" "Nope," He said, "Go back." I thought to myself, *I was just coming to the beach today to relax in the sun with my hun.* Nope!

I humbled myself and started walking back. One of the girls said, "Oh look, here she comes again." I was embarrassed and thought to myself, *Lord, you'd better show up when I get there. I am almost 50 years old walking over to hang out with a group of young college students. They don't want me coming over again!* I approached, smiling, all the while praying for grace and mercy. I crouched down in the same spot and said, "Well, this may be the second craziest thing that happens to you today. The Lord wants me to offer to pray over all of you and give encouragement." In that moment, a few of the kids who were not present at my first visit returned.

The alpha girl came over. It was obvious she was ruling the roost. I felt like I was in a teen musical. She came over to me and with a firm, stern voice of protection she demanded, "Who are you?" Before I had time to think, my introduction rolled off my tongue in a way I had never introduced myself before. "Hi, my name is Debbie and I am a born again believer in Jesus Christ." I thought to myself, *What is going on!* She asked, "What do you want?" I replied, "The Lord told me to come and pray over your group and offer you all encouragement." She looked around the entire circle, looked back over to me, and said, "Well, if we're gonna do this, let's do it right." I am not making this up. This actually happened. Not only did she command everyone to stand for prayer, she insisted that everyone hold hands. On a public beach!

Yes, that's right, twenty-some young folks stood in a circle holding hands, waiting to receive a blessing. I was blown away! Now my husband was watching in the distance. As I prayed, the Lord spoke through me. It was so much; I can't remember everything. But here's what I do remember: He explained His love for them and encouraged them to seek Him. He finished by telling them to make a difference in the world through Him, and reassured them there is nothing they could do that is unforgivable. When He was done, and I say He because the words that came out of my mouth were all from Him, they all said, "Amen!" and clapped. Yes, they all clapped! They all thanked me and with blessings, we parted ways.

This is just one story of many which illustrates that when we obey, God shows up and shows off. We have to be able to hear Him. This was an audible, "God is with me," *hearing from God* moment.

Positioning ourselves to be able to hear from God is vital to our Christian walk.

God challenges us to ask Him, and He's going to answer us:

> "Call to Me and I will answer you, and I will tell you great and mighty things, which you do not know." (Jeremiah 33:3)

"I will instruct you and teach you in the way you should go. I will counsel you with my eye upon you. Do not be as the horse or as the mule which have no understanding, whose trappings include bit and bridle to hold them in check, Otherwise they will not come near to you." (Psalm 32:8,9)

"Trust in the LORD with all your heart and do not lean on your own understanding. In all your ways acknowledge Him, and He will make your paths straight." (Proverbs 3:5,6)

"Your word is a lamp to my feet and a light to my path." (Psalm 119:105)

Some of us may feel as though we don't hear from God, or that God doesn't speak to us. Hebrews 4:12 says, "For the word of God is living and active and sharper than any two-edged sword, and piercing as far as the division of soul and spirit, of both joints and marrow, and able to judge the thoughts and intentions of the heart."

Do you hear from God? Do you struggle with knowing whose voice you're tuning in to? Do you feel as though God has never spoken to you? Rest assured the God of the universe, who has taken up residence in you, desires to speak to you.

John 10:27 may be the most important verse for learning how to position ourselves to meditate and hear God. It says, "My sheep hear my voice, and I know them, and they follow me." I go into my quiet place so I can hear from God. The Holy Spirit of God speaks to me in my thought process. He either compels or restrains me, and I've learned to feel, know, and sense His hand on me. Oftentimes I will unload on God. If I'm stuck or struggling with something, I'll say, "Lord, I need a word from You. I need You to speak to me." Then I take my Bible and wait for a verse to come to my mind or I do a random flip-open.

A flip-open is when the Lord leads my hand to a verse that will encourage or guide me. I'm telling you, ten out of ten times, He gives me the right verse. My mind has to be in a place to receive. So if I'm struggling with something and the Lord leads me to a Scripture reference that convicts me, I must be willing to receive that. I will process that with God, and repent if necessary. It's important that we trust the movement of God. He said greater is He that is in us, than he who is in the world.[9] He lives and moves within our beings. How important it is to know that He is working things out within us.

One day, I was asking God to help me be more like Him. My flip-open was, "He must increase, but I must decrease." (John 3:30) I lost it! I sobbed for an hour. Those few words changed my life. Conviction straight to my heart—I must decrease. For me, this meant I needed to get out of His way; I needed to allow Him to have His way in my life.

When my oldest daughter started kindergarten, we were all so excited and proud of her. However, her absence was very noticeable. I was uncomfortable when I noticed that she and her siblings had started to disconnect. Over time, my heart ached for answers. One night in December, my husband and I were talking before bed. I shared my heart with him, but he wasn't exactly getting what I was trying to communicate. I was frustrated with myself, wondering why I was in such torment over this.

He was retiring for the evening, and I just wasn't settled. I needed to be still. I got down on my knees by the edge of the bed and started praying and crying out to God for insight, understanding, answers—anything. After about an hour and a half, my husband finally intervened and said, "He heard you, come to bed." I said, "I am not getting up until He answers me or releases me."

Fast forward, here's how my answer came. A week or two later, my daughter came home from school sobbing. She missed us so much, she wanted to be homeschooled. She insisted she did not want to go back to school. We asked her where she heard about being homeschooled. We were puzzled. We barely knew anything about it ourselves. How or why she came up with that was a mystery. Or so we thought.

My husband and I sat her down and gently asked her questions to investigate what brought this on. We felt her answers were pure hearted

---

[9] 1 John 4:4

and that no harm had come to her; maybe she was just confused and a little homesick. We reassured her school was fun and she would miss her new friends and teacher.

She came home and cried every day for weeks. We continued to ask questions. We were reassured she was safe. Puzzled with this unknown issue, we wondered what we should do.

The Holy Spirit reminded me of the time I knelt beside the bed, begging for answers. My plea and heart's desire was for my family to be connected and stay together. He revealed that my daughter's mysterious need to come home and her request to be homeschooled was His answer.

I hadn't been quite sure exactly what was missing, but this was the answer. It was unbelievable! I wrestled a little about the decision, but sensed this was God's doing. I was sold on it. My husband, not so much. He was not liking the idea and wasn't comfortable with it. My daughter cried more. I told her that if she felt like the Lord was leading us to do this, we both needed to pray and ask Him to change Daddy's heart. We prayed and meditated on God's promises.

Two months later, the son of our good friends lost the privilege of attending private school two months before school ended for the summer. Our friend came to us asking for advice on what he should do for his son. As he shared some options of different schools, all of a sudden my husband offered for me to homeschool his son for the remainder of the year! I laughed and asked, "What are you talking about?" Crazy, right? Don't ever underestimate God's sense of humor. Well, we made the decision to help them. We called the school and received instructions on what he needed from me to help him finish out his school year. It was a success. It also set my husband up for me to bring my daughter home.

Shortly after we committed to bringing her home, my husband's work schedule changed to shift work. Had she stayed in school, my husband would have had very little time with her. God was moving and shifting us to fulfill my heart's desire to preserve my family.

I truly believe that if I had not sat still and pressed in for so long, I would have stayed tormented and stuck in my own mind. I never would have had the opportunity to see the hand of God move in such a huge way for us. God has taught me through His faithfulness to seek Him for all of my needs. The more He answers my prayers, the more I pray and rely on Him. By intentionally posturing ourselves to hear from God, it gives pause and allows the Word to minister to our minds, hearts, and souls. He is our strength and the light to our path.

A huge burden of mine that I seek the Lord for is in preparation for the women's events that I lead. I spend months in prayer and fasting, pressing in to ask God what He desires our time together to look like. This book is the result of what He gave me for *The Be Still and Know that I Am God* Revival. **Remember, meditation is a necessity, not an option.** Remember the lack of meditation is a spiritual trap.

I can't say it enough—God desires to move us and to use us for His purpose. This is why we have to be in tune to hear from Him. We don't want to miss out on the opportunities He genuinely wants to give us. There is power in His activity that we do not have access to without Him. Check out this next God-story. It was the perfect answer to a problem that was burdening a friend's heart. God gave her exactly what she needed.

I was driving home from shopping when I felt the Holy Spirit compelling me to take an alternate route home. There was no detour, so there was really no need for me to take the longer route. It was illogical to take that way home, yet I found myself following His instructions to make the turn. Five miles into driving down a long, empty road, I saw a van and what looked like reporters looking up a tree. The scene was very strange.

The Holy Spirit said, "Pull over and ask them what's in the tree." I wondered, R*eally?* I looked up into the tree thinking maybe there was a bear, or a cougar, or something else big and wild. I pulled over, rolled my window down, and yelled across the street, "You all ok?" They answered, "Yes thank you, we're fine." OK, good. I asked, "So what's in the tree?" "Gypsy moths," they said. "We're doing a report on how gypsy moths are destroying the natural habitat in the local area and killing thousands of trees." Bingo! This was mind blowing.

Why is this important? My friend had recently told me how bad the gypsy moths were. She was upset about all the trees she was losing and felt like she needed to bring awareness to someone that could help control them. She lived about five more miles up the road from where the reporters were investigating.

The Lord answered my friend's concern by prompting me in His perfect timing to drive by the reporters at just the right time. Of course, I immediately took the opportunity to ask them, "Do you guys have some time? I have a friend who would love to give you a story." I led them to her house, introduced them, and drove away, saying to myself, "But God!" Super cool! Now, I realize some may say that was just a coincidence. I don't believe in coincidences. My God is all seeing, all knowing, all able to do whatever He likes. If we listen to His voice, follow His promptings, and allow Him to guide us, He will use us to get the job done. I have many God-stories just like this one which prove He is a God who hears us and speaks to us.

How about you? I'm sure you have a story or two that you just can't explain. Maybe you've never realized it could be God's hand making it all happen. I have to tell you, yes! Yes! It is from God! From this point on, look for Him. Listen to Him. Follow Him! The Holy Spirit will guide and direct you.

Pause: Have you noticed that when you obey what God asks you to do, it doesn't only bless you, it blesses Him too. It's a win-win situation.

I believe the Lord communicates with us all day long. We will see and hear Him if we practice being in His presence. What am I saying? It doesn't mean you're out of His presence. It means you **practice understanding that His presence is ever with you.**

My husband and I recently went to Israel. I had many expectations of what I would do, how I would act, and how I would respond emotionally. I was actually going to visit the same significant historical places that Jesus Himself once walked! I really thought that when I got to the Western (Wailing) Wall in Jerusalem, I would be compelled to pray and sob because that is what I have seen others do. However, when I got there, I came to see and understand the reason why many prayed at the wall, and my mind was changed.

The Western Wall is so significant because most religious Jewish folks believe it is the one place on earth to be close to God, in His presence. This broke my heart, because the reality is that God lives in us. He takes up residence in us when we accept Jesus Christ as our Lord and Savior.[10] I realize that generally, the Jewish people do not acknowledge Jesus as the Messiah. But for those of us who are born again believers, we don't need to go to a wall to be in His presence. I am so appreciative that I can be in His presence anywhere, any time.

Many who inhabit Jerusalem, and more who come from all over the world, gravitate to the Western Wall out of love for God and a great desire to be in His presence. How much more should we, as His children, give up our busyness to seek His presence? He has made it easy for us. He is always with us. We don't have to go far to have a date night with Jesus!

Often we do a lot of asking, a lot of demanding, and a lot of complaining, but we don't spend enough time to really hear from God on the resolutions of those things. David went up into the hills, into the mountains, and into the caves. He got away from it all and spent that time with God. I think many people are hesitant to believe they can hear from God because they aren't sure whether it's God speaking, themselves speaking, or if it's the enemy setting a trap. I want to remind you that He says, "My sheep hear my voice." You know when He speaks-you just know. You know because it resonates and you wouldn't normally tell yourself to do good, to lay down your rights, to apologize, to sit and wait, etc., or to take an alternative route for no apparent reason.

Pause: "The Lord is my shepherd, I shall not want" (Psalm 23:1) and "My sheep hear my voice." (John 10:27)

Just take in this truth: "My sheep hear my voice and I know them, and they follow me." There's a song by Casting Crowns called "The Voice of Truth." The words are so significant. It brings to mind the struggles we have. What I've learned in my training with the Lord is

---

[10] 2 Corinthians 13:15

44

that when I press in, the first voice I hear is always His. Just remember, "My sheep hear my voice. I know them, and they follow me." Keep this in mind; His voice will never contradict His Word. Trust in His Word.

Are you at all troubled or concerned about meditating? The Holy Spirit is going to lead and guide you. You can't constantly worry about being set up to fall into a spiritual trap. When you know God and you have the Holy Spirit within you, He says, "My sheep hear my voice." Go to your quiet place and listen for it. You will miss out if you don't. Yes, the enemy's going to want to steal from you and set you up, but here's the thing—if you're not meditating on God, you're already snared in his trap. Do you understand that? *If you're not spending that time with God, you are already at a loss.* Instead of living the abundant life you desire, your life is lacking. Has something kept you back from meditating? Is it fear? Lack of time? Something else? Do you think meditation is not biblical? I'd like to challenge this mindset. Your spiritual life depends on it! You can be set free. Satan uses misinformation to keep us from the good things God has for us.

Various religions have their own reasons, styles, and steps in meditation. They may use the same words and desire the same results, but rest assured if they are not praying to the God of the Holy Bible, it is not biblical meditation. This shows the importance of how much we need to know our God, how much we need to know the truth of God's Word, and how much we need to live it out. Biblical meditation is not asking you to go into a trance-like mindless state. Never! Biblical meditation invites you to press in with God by being still and thinking upon Him. Meditation was God's idea, He designed it. It predates any other religions; you can trace it back to its origin in the Old Testament Scriptures with Joshua 1:8.

I think many people have seen the great benefits of Christian meditation through the years. Those who are not Christ followers desire those benefits and have come up with their own way of manufacturing similar results. The results we will get from our obedience are far more accurate and valuable than any other form of meditation. Hands down, God's way is the best way.

Are you beginning to see how vital it is to hear God? The God of the universe speaks to us and invites us into His kingdom work. Can you believe it? *As His ambassadors, if we are too busy and distracted to hear Him, how much ministry do we miss out on? This is a detrimental spiritual trap. It affects the outcomes of others.*

Have you ever felt compelled to pray, to call someone, to bless someone with money, to deliver a meal, or to stop by and see someone? That is God prompting you. He's inviting you to be a part of His bigger plan. When we obey, we normally get comments like:

- "I can't believe you just called me!"
- "I can't believe you gifted me!"
- "I was praying asking God to help me."
- "I was asking God to show Himself real to me."

It's amazing to be a part of His work! There is nothing, nothing more exciting than serving our King.

If you feel you have yet to hear from God, ask Him. Tell Him you'd like to hear from Him. Give Him the opportunity to speak into your life. His voice is always positive. In times of correction, it is always supported by His love. God's voice is never negative or condemning. Never! That is of the enemy.

God speaks to us in a variety of ways. He may use a random stranger to speak into your life. He can use a billboard on the side of the road. He can give you a word, an answer, or direction all through a program on the radio or TV. He can reach you wherever you are.

> *"Ask, and it will be given to you; seek, and you will find; knock, and it will be opened to you."*
>
> *Matthew 7:7*

CHAPTER 5

THE ART OF BEING STILL

I t is of great importance to God that we take time out for Him and for ourselves. There are multiple commands throughout Scripture for us to rest. Jesus invites us in Matthew 11:28, "Come to me, all you who are weary and burdened, and I will give you rest."

Do you struggle with sitting still? Many people do. It's a discipline to take the time out of our busy schedules to sit and seem to "do nothing," as our minds tell us. But sitting still for the Lord is so much more than doing nothing. It's an investment. Many of us feel great pressure to keep up the ball of responsibility rolling. If you're in ministry, it is that much more essential to sit at Jesus' feet and get your instructions from Him. If you don't, it can become an entity of doing, rather than being. It is no mistake that we are called human beings, not human doings. You must balance your responsibilities. When they are out of balance, you surely will be too. Being still is a daily practice for your benefit.

We should identify the source of our need to keep busy. Is it fear of being unproductive, lazy, not accepted, lonely or running from life and our thoughts? Do we fill our silence with a lot of empty words because we're uncomfortable with quiet? Do we understand our need to be healed, to be at rest, to have clarity, and to think clearly? We need to be set free from our own thoughts, especially those that are negative. It is important that healing comes. We need to purge, declutter, eliminate noise, and give up control to trust God. Psalm 1:2 says, "But his delight is in the law of the LORD, and in His law he meditates day and night."

Jesus often left the multitudes to be alone and to be still with the Father. His example alone should drive us to the place of meditation. *Being still is not an hour during church service. It is developing a relationship with Jesus every day of the week.*

In order to meditate, we need to learn how to slow down and be still. We know Psalm 46:10 says, "Be still, and know that I am God." What does it mean to be still? *"Be still" means to be free of chaos and crazy living.* Through my experience ministering to women, I find that most struggle with this. In the day and age we live in, there is a lack of encouragement to be still. Instead, there is great pressure to keep the ball rolling, so to speak.

Pause: Are you exhausted from trying to keep the ball rolling rather than trusting in the One responsible for rolling the ball? This reinforces why it's so important to master how to rest and be still in the Lord.

So, how can we learn to be still? When should we start to be still? Where do we go to be still? What are the benefits of being still? Let's turn our attention to Luke 10:38-42. As we read, I encourage you to really analyze this. Which character do you associate with most? How would you respond in this situation?

> Now as they were traveling along, He entered a village; and a woman named Martha welcomed Him into her home. She had a sister called Mary, who was seated at the Lord's feet, listening to His word. But Martha was distracted with all her preparations; and she came up to Him and said, "Lord, do You not care that my sister has left me to do all the serving alone? Then tell her to help me." But the Lord answered and said to her, "Martha, Martha, you are worried and bothered about so many things; but only one thing is necessary, for Mary has chosen the good part, which shall not be taken away from her.

I'm sure we've all heard sermons and the different perspectives that can come from these verses. We're going to keep it very simple. We're just going to go by what the Word says.

See what Martha says to Jesus. "Don't you care that I'm doing all this work by myself and she's sitting here at your feet? Tell her to get up and help me." Let's think about that. She's stressed, she's overwhelmed, she's not thinking straight because she's so encumbered with her tasks. Notice it? A spiritual trap. She's missing out on the most important thing in the room. She's thinking she has to be a good steward and hostess. "I've got to prepare a meal. After all, Jesus is here!" Martha is hounded with the pressures of life. Notice her mind is running off with her emotions. She's thinking, "I have to keep the ball rolling."

Do you agree that we tend to allow responsibilities to control our lives? Many of us think, "We have to be responsible Christians. We have to be good stewards of what God's given us." Yes, that is so true. But there was a point in time on this day that Jesus sat down to talk. One woman decided to listen, to sit at His feet and be still. And the other woman chose to be busy. Jesus says, "Martha, Martha, you are worried and bothered about so many things." Now we know the Bible says we are not to worry about anything. And He's telling her, "You're worrying and fussing." Yet another spiritual trap. "But there's only one thing you need, Martha." What is that one thing Martha needs?

Think about the many times you may have been in Martha's shoes. Remember the tone of your voice, the attitude of your heart, and your frustration. You felt overwhelmed and unappreciated as your efforts seemed to go unrecognized. It appeared no one was grateful for what you were doing. Everyone else was just sitting around the table enjoying each other's company. No one offered to help you.

Let's consider this is how Martha was feeling. The problem is that she demanded that Jesus take action against her sister. Could she have been jealous or overly controlling? We're not quite sure. But the one thing we are sure of is Jesus' response. He told her, "Martha, there's only one thing that you need. Mary has chosen what is better. And it is not to be taken away from her."

Notice what Jesus said to Martha. Mary has me, and she chose the better! I wonder if that infuriated her even more. He reinforced Mary's choice. He protected her from feeling as though she was in the wrong. He was thrilled that Mary's heart was to sit with Him and be filled. One might notice that in Martha's need for control, it would appear in this moment she was too consumed with duty over relationship.

There is a point to make here that each of us needs to serve, and each needs to sit at the feet of Jesus. Meditating will help us find our own personal balance and our heart motives—why do we do what we do?

The most important thing for us to understand is that Jesus wants this time with us. He wants us to press in. Honestly, this speaks volumes for all relationships. How many of us miss out on relationships because we're too busy? How much more valuable are our relationships than the tasks that demand our attention? It can be hard, especially when we have multiple responsibilities. Maybe we can restructure the way we prepare our day to make time for the Lord. After all, being still and meditating on Jesus is clearly the better choice. Can we be like Mary? Can we refuse to let anything interrupt our time with Him?

You may be saying, "OK. How do I do that?" Honestly, you may need to figure this out on your own. It may be different for each person. For instance, I had to learn to give up control. You, too, may need to release control. I believe Martha was a control freak. Many of us tend to be control freaks only because we have so many responsibilities. But when the attitude of our heart gets to a place where we demand help, and we rebuke Jesus because we want Him to reprimand someone else, we need to take a time out.

Control had gripped Martha's heart. Be honest with yourself. Does any of this resonate with you? Do you need to learn to give up control? It's something to think about. I know it may be hard, but it is crucial. Can you commit to taking 30 minutes with God every day as a start? Choosing to shut out the world is a great first step.

Do you know that faith is having the courage to let God have control? Hear me on this as well. This is not a "must-do check off my list" item that is required of us, it is an exhortation; it's the better choice. It should come from a growing desire to know Him more, rather than "let me do this and get it over with." Again, it's about the postu_ Devotions, meditations, and attending church services sh_ because "I have to in order to be a 'good' Christian." Because w value and benefit, it should be *"I long for, I desire to, I cannot **not** s_ time with Him; it is just that important to me."* Do you see the difference:

We must admit our busyness. Have you heard this acronym for B.U.S.Y?

Being

Under

Satan's

Yoke

Clearly, being too busy is a spiritual trap. It's shocking to realize how distracted we are from God in our daily lives. Can you see your need to slow down? If so, confess your need for control. You can get your thoughts in submission by meditating on God's Word.

Oftentimes, I have found that when I have made time to be still with God in a busy day, He has stretched and multiplied time for me elsewhere. I think it's a matter of learning to truly trust Him. When we desire to meditate and learn how to be still, this verse, the greatest commandment of them all, comes to my mind: "And you shall love the Lord your God with all your heart, and with all your soul, and with all your mind, and with all your strength." (Mark 12:30)

If you're going to love God with all your heart, there won't be a whole lot of room for anything else in there. He says, "Above all else, guard your heart." (Proverbs 4:23 NIV) Psalm 51:10 says, "Create in me a clean heart, O God, and renew a right spirit within me."(KJV) How do we love God with all of our hearts? We can make God the priority by decluttering the mess of the idols of our heart. An idol is anything we value more than God. Matthew 6:21 says, "Where your treasure is, there your heart will be also." What consumes your thoughts, time, energy and finances? If you are more dedicated to anything than your pursuit of God and pleasing Him, it might be an idol.

51

Praying the scriptures will quiet and calm your soul—remember sitting by the still waters. He restores our soul. Sometimes diseases of the soul are more dangerous than those of the body. We have to be aware of what's going on in and around us.

Then, of course, He says to love Him with all of your mind. This is key. To love Him with all of your mind, you first need peace of mind; a mindset shift of understanding that you can't be thinking of a hundred million things. Your mind has to be steadfast on Him. As I mentioned, Brother Lawrence calls it practicing His presence. *It's about intentionally fixing your mind on God, continuing in His presence and experiencing His peace.*

God tells us in Isaiah 26:3, "Thou will keep him in perfect peace, whose mind is stayed on Thee: because he trusteth in Thee." (KJV) Think about that. Put on the mind of Christ.

How do you love God with all of your mind? Memorizing and meditating on the Scriptures is the perfect start. How do you love Him with all of your soul? Meditating on the Scriptures. How do you love Him with all of your heart? Meditating on the Scriptures. The answers are getting easier than the questions!

Meditation is diving deep into the Word. We can't just read the Bible. We have to understand it, apply it, be empowered by it, and recognize how necessary the Word is for personal transformation. We are all on a journey. The God of the universe wants your journey to be amazing. He gives you the tools and equips you to do it. It's up to you to apply it.

Lastly, we are to love God with all our strength. Where do we get our strength? From the Lord. Psalm 28:7 says, "The Lord is my strength and my shield. In Him my heart trusts and I am helped." Scripture says the joy of the Lord is my strength[11]. My flesh and my heart may fail but God is the strength of my heart and my portion forever[12].

How do we renew our strength? By waiting upon the Lord. "But they that wait upon the Lord shall renew their strength; they shall

---

[11] Nehemiah 8:10
[12] Psalm 73:26

mount up with wings as eagles; they shall run, and not be weary; and they shall walk, and not faint." (Isaiah 40:31 KJV)

To mount up with the ability to soar: "They shall run and not be weary, and they shall walk and not faint." Look here! We shall run—that isn't being idle or slow or constantly being still; it says we will run and not be weary! Are you running through life now? Are you weary? Why? This is huge! Do you see it? You don't want to miss this!

Being still gives us the power to run and not grow weary. We gird up for the race that is set before us by meditating. Meditation is our fueling station. We can enter into a lifestyle of meditation by first learning how to be still and love the Lord our God with all of our heart, soul, mind, and strength. It starts with the Scriptures. We will run and not be weary. We won't grow faint. There is so much truth in this one verse.

Do you see the action steps God is asking us to take? Renew your mind. Renew your strength. Renew a right spirit within me. Create in me a clean heart. Wow, wow, wow! I just love it. The truth will set you free!

The challenge is to ask yourself, "Do I love the Lord my God with all of my heart?" What's in your heart? Is it jealousy? Bitterness? Anger? Unforgiveness? Are you struggling within yourself? *Those are all spiritual traps.* Does your flesh need to be in check? Because you can't love Him with *all* your heart if you haven't done the maintenance work on the flesh. You can't love Him with *all* your heart if part of your heart has been taken over by sin or idols.

Maybe we need a time of confession and repentance. I have made confession and repentance a part of my daily quiet time with God. I truly want my heart to be surrendered to His authority. I don't want unconfessed sin to hold me back from communing with my God. Do we truly love God with all of our hearts? What are we willing to give up to allow that to happen?

I've seen God move in the most illogical ways on my behalf. I grew up as a seasonal camper at the New Jersey shore. I loved the environment and my summertime friends, some of whom I still consider friends to this day. I have fond memories of camping. Little did I know that I would also raise my kids as seasonal campers.

We eventually became seasonal campers at Sandy Cove, our favorite Christian retreat center. We love the diversity, biblical teaching, life-long connections, and the atmosphere that encourages us to be still. I use these summers away as a sabbatical, or hiatus, mainly due to what the Lord taught me during my two-year "wilderness experience." I find it very important to honor God with what He has taught me in meditating on Him and maintaining a life of practicing His presence.

Throughout the year I'm very involved in pouring into others through counseling, coaching, leading women's ministry events, and teaching Bible studies. These ministries keep me very busy over and above my family responsibilities. This time away is a cherished time for me and God. God has blessed me with a godly husband who supports me and understands my need to spend this time alone with Jesus out of obedience. He not only gets it, he benefits from my experience—His wife is changing and becoming more like Jesus.

I realize not everyone may be able to get away with Jesus in quite the same way. Nor does everyone require such a substantial amount of time away with God. I encourage you to do what works best for you— maybe take a personal day or a weekend retreat— in order to carve out time with Him.

We need to nourish our souls! The Word of God is the perfect nutrient.

We have to take care of ourselves. Spiritual and physical wellness are so important in our meditation. What do you feel you are lacking? Do you desire more out of your walk with the Lord? How will you achieve that? Are you willing to commit to that in order to make it happen?

I encourage you to answer these questions for yourself and consider adding being still as one of your action steps to take on your journey in drawing closer to God.

But his delight is in the law of the LORD, and
in His law he meditates day and night.

Psalm 1:2

CHAPTER 6

BIBLE STUDY AND JOURNALING

The Word of God gives us everything pertaining to life and godliness. It is alive and active. Do we understand the power of the Scriptures? They transform a heart, a mind, a life—my life, your life! The Word of God is so powerful. We can't begin to understand all of it. When we seek more of God and His truth, the Holy Spirit will guide us. We will begin to grow and develop the closer walk with the Lord Jesus that we desire.

If you want to see a shift, your mindset has to change. 1 Chronicles 16:11 says, "Seek the Lord and His strength. Seek His presence continually." Again, Psalm 1:2 says, "But his delight is in the law of the Lord, and in His law he meditates day and night." Your mindset will change through studying the Word of God, memorizing it, and meditating on it. It will renew your mind and restore your soul.

> Psalm 19:7-10
> The law of the Lord is perfect, restoring the soul;
> The testimony of the Lord is sure, making wise the simple.
> The precepts of the Lord are right, rejoicing the heart;
> The commandment of the Lord is pure, enlightening the eyes.
> The fear of the Lord is clean, enduring forever;
> The judgments of the Lord are true; they are righteous altogether.

> They are more desirable than gold, yes, than much fine gold;
> Sweeter also than honey and the drippings of the honeycomb.

Praying, meditating, being still, hearing from God, journaling, and Bible memorization are all great practices. Bible study is essential for learning, growing, and transforming us to be more like Christ. John 1:1-5 tells us why:

> "In the beginning was the Word, and the Word was with God, and the Word was God. He was in the beginning with God. All things came into being through Him, and apart from Him nothing came into being that has come into being. In Him was life, and the life was the Light of men. The Light shines in the darkness, and the darkness did not comprehend it."

Matthew 6:21 says, "for where your treasure is, there your heart will be also." This is where my heart is. How about you? Understanding that this is not the primary concept of this verse, it is still fitting for how we could approach Bible study. "The kingdom of heaven is like a treasure hidden in the field, which a man found and hid again; and from joy over it he goes and sells all that he has and buys that field." (Matthew 13:44)

Bible study is like a treasure hunt for me. I am an explorer by nature. I love to dig deep to find the jewels of God's Word for myself. I can spend hours on rabbit trails. I get so excited about all the truth just waiting to be discovered.

Studying the Bible and journaling my findings is my all-time favorite way to meditate on the Lord. I love it! I'm addicted to learning the Bible. I've hungered and thirsted for more since I became a believer 26 years ago. I can't stress enough the importance of being in your Bible daily.

In the parable above, the man sold everything he had to buy the field because he knew it held treasure. What are you willing to give up to discover the many treasures hidden in the Scriptures? **I will say it**

again: Bible study is a necessity, not an option, to navigate through life here on earth.

God exhorts us, "Study to shew thyself approved unto God, a workman that needeth not to be ashamed, rightly dividing the word of truth." (2 Timothy 2:15) Many people ask which is the best Bible translation to use. I personally like the KJV, NASB, and NLT. As the old adage says, "the best translation is the one that is read." It's important to not only read the Scriptures, but to comprehend and apply them. I suggest using a concordance (I use www.blueletterbible.org), a pen, and a notebook. Here are some ways you can study the Bible:

- study the Bible verse by verse through chapters
- study a particular theme or book of the Bible
- do a word search: comb through the Scriptures and discover everything God has said about a particular word
- Read multiple Scriptures on a topic
- Inductive Marking System (explained below)

You may not feel you have any free time; I encourage you to start off with maybe just 30 minutes to read and meditate on God's Word. The deep truths God reveals in His Word will blow your mind!

There are times when I have read a verse a hundred times. Then on the hundred-and-first time, God reveals a new truth to me. When you are given a divine eye-opener to a verse you read, how often you will say, "Wow, I never saw that before!" The Bible is not a straightforward message like a regular man-written book. It is inspired by God Himself! It has over 40 authors; their words flow together through God's inspiration. Many people have tried to find errors but have come up empty—there are no errors. His divine inspiration is powerful and perfect. The more you read and study your Bible, the more you will come to know.

Inductive Bible Study

The Inductive Marking System is based on four key principles: *Observation, Interpretation, Application, and Transformation.*

Observation – What do I "see" in Scripture – what does it say? When reading the Bible, observing the text should lead us to the interpretation of the text. It is a means to an end, not an end in and of itself.

Interpretation – What did the author intend for this to mean?

Application – How does the meaning of the text apply to my life? How do I live this out? The goal of Bible study is to apply it to your life. It will transform you! "For if anyone is a hearer of the word and not a doer, he is like a man who looks at his natural face in a mirror; for once he has looked at himself and gone away, he has immediately forgotten what kind of person he was. But one who looks intently at the perfect law, the law of liberty, and abides by it, not having become a forgetful hearer but an effectual doer, this man will be blessed in what he does." (James 1:23-25)

Transformation – How has what I observed, interpreted, and applied changed me? *Transformation comes when our teacher, the Holy Spirit, allows us to receive a new awareness of the truth and we apply it.* Transformation is a mindset shift. Our eyes and hearts are opened to a concept that resonates with the power of God's Word to work in and through us.

Have you noticed that as you read, your mind often skips over the little words because it thinks it knows what they are? As a result, you don't always take in what you're actually reading. The premise of the Inductive Marking System is that you read and acknowledge the importance of every word.

It has been stated by those who use the method of Inductive Bible Study that it's not just for information, but also for transformation. I agree. There are many inductive methods out there on the shelves. I personally enjoy Kay Arthur's method. I have used this for both my own personal study and for the women's Bible study I lead. To keep everyone in unison, we use the NASB version.

As we begin to mark the text, words begin jumping off the page. It's amazing and addicting. It's enlightening to see new truths in the Scripture passages that we have read several times before. There are many "light bulb" moments. Bible study is probably one of the most beneficial ways to meditate and grow because the Bible is the Word of God.

Remember what mediation means. It means to go deep, to really think about it, to ponder it. I encourage you to really study your Bible. Pull it apart and ask yourself some good questions:

- Who is the author?
- Who is the author speaking to?
- What words are reoccurring in the text?
- Is there a command or a warning?

Be an investigator of the Word. Ask yourself WHO, WHEN, WHERE, WHY, HOW? You are an inspector of the Word. You will hold forth the truth that will be proven by collecting your data. That's what the Bereans did.

Memorization is a vital part of studying the Word. "Your Word have I hidden in my heart that I may not sin against you." (Psalm 119:11 NKJV) So dig deep, get excited, prove the Word, and let it transform your life.

God says when we hunger and thirst, He fills us. Believe that you will get an amazing filling by hungering after the Word. You may appreciate curling up on the couch with your Bible and a cup of coffee or tea. I love reading my Bible on the beach. I offer these suggestions because they have worked for me personally. It's a personal relationship that is unique for each individual. With great encouragement, I challenge you to incorporate something that gives you time and space to be alone with God. Be creative. Enjoy Him!

Don't neglect this privilege of meeting with God in His Word. *That is the key. It is essential.*

As we wrap up the importance of Bible study, allow me to show you another interesting thought. As we study the Scriptures, we learn so much of who God is, who we are, and who we are not. Learning the names of God teaches us who He is. He is the essence of all His characteristics. God doesn't only have the emotion of love, He *is* love. He is the very word that describes Himself. This is so deep.

Do we take the time out to really to get to know God? The verse in Psalms says, "Be still and know that I am God." Let's flip that. Before you can be still, maybe you need to know Him more?

Know that I am God and be still.

Here are some examples of the person and character of God:

- ELOHIM- "God's power and might" Genesis 1:1, Psalm 19:1
- ADONAI- "Lord", a reference to the Lordship of God. Malachi 1:6
- JEHOVAH-YAHWEH- "God's divine salvation" Genesis 2:4
- JEHOVAH-ROHI- "The Lord my shepherd" Psalm 23:1
- JEHOVAH-RAPHA- "The Lord our healer" Exodus 15:26
- JEHOVAH-TSIDKENU- "The Lord our righteousness" Jeremiah 23:6
- JEHOVAH-JIREH- "The Lord will provide" Genesis 22:13-14
- JEHOVAH-SHALOM- "The Lord is peace" Judges 6:24
- EL-ELYON- "The most high God" Genesis 14:17-20, Isaiah 14:13-14
- EL-ROI- "The strong one who sees" Genesis 16:13
- EL-SHADDAI- "The God of the mountains or God Almighty" Genesis 17:1, Psalm 91:1
- EL-OLAM- "The everlasting God" Isaiah 40:28-31
- LAMB OF God- John 1:29
- LIFE- John 14:6
- LIGHT OF THE WORLD- John 8:12
- LORD God ALMIGHTY- Revelation 15:3
- LORD God OF HOSTS- Jeremiah 15:16

- LORD JESUS CHRIST- 1 Corinthians 15:57
- LORD OF ALL- Acts 10:36
- LORD OF GLORY- 1 Corinthians 2:8
- LOVE- 1 John 4:8
- LOVINGKINDNESS- Psalm 144:2

God is omnipotent. He is all-powerful, He directs the weather, the seasons, gravity, etc.

God is omnipresent. He is everywhere. He is always with us. He was, is and always will be.

God is omniscient. He is all-knowing. He is aware of the past, present, and future. He existed before the worlds were created.

Jesus never fails! God is the essence of all His promises. His promises teach us that we can trust Him, that He has our best interest at heart, that He is with us, for us, and loves us. We begin to shift our mindset when we meditate on who He is and what He has promised. God does not lie. He can't break His promises. Knowing this enables us to be still before Him because we just can't get enough! *Meditating on knowing God will change your life, your mindset, your attitude, and your desires.* It will give you a new perspective on why you are here on earth and enable you to grow in your love for Him.

Pause: God is always near; we are the ones who move away from Him. As you start to identify what is holding you back from spending time with God, now is the time to release it. Today is a new day. Are you committed to knowing God more? Of course you are. I want to encourage you to get your calendar out now and schedule yourself a consistent date time with you and Jesus. Try it for just one week. Start small and watch it grow. You will be glad you did.

Journaling is another great way to engage in meditation with God.

Journaling is a great exercise. It gives you the opportunity to look back and read where you were, where you are now, and where you're going. For some, journaling may be the right tool for us to record our thoughts, the things we ponder on most, and our reflections. Journal your desires, your hopes, your wants; pour it all out to God. Journal your Bible studies and the verses that speak to you the most. Maybe, like me, you need to write out what you are reading.

I often find myself journaling what the Holy Spirit shares with me in secret. You can journal your prayers and record the answers as they come. I love to journal. It really is a great release for me. It forces me to sit down. I enjoy journaling what I am grateful for as I ponder all the good things that God is doing in my life. Try it.

When God gives you a word, direction, wisdom, or instructions, you will want to write it down immediately. Trust me. The older I get, the faster I lose what He says, even if I repeat it multiple times. Writing it down shows Daddy how important He is to us and that we don't want to forget what He has to say.

Do you like to journal? I know, not everyone does. Would you accept a challenge? Try it! Get a journal. Start by jotting down five things you're thankful for every day. Add a prayer concern. List questions you would like God to answer for you. Think about the great things He has done for you. Get in the practice of recording your time with Him through journaling. You never know, you may love it! Record what He shares with you in secret.

Your relationship with God is your most important relationship. You need to intentionally nurture this relationship by setting aside time with Him daily. *If you don't sacrifice for what you want, what you want becomes the sacrifice.* We don't want that to happen with God. Intentional means an action performed with awareness. It's done deliberately, consciously, and on purpose. Our quiet time with God needs to be proactive. Try reading Psalm 46:10 like this: "I will be still and know You are God." We should really do that. Learning to be still and silent positions us just to BE. *To be still in the Hebrew means to let down or to cease from frantic activity to relax, just be.*

With that said, I use my summers to rest from my typically busy schedule. When I begin my summer sabbatical, I buy a new journal as I enter into a time of being still. I prepare myself to rest at the feet of Jesus. I spend a lot of time sitting under amazing biblical teaching and worship. This is where I press in like Mary. I spend a lot of time meditating and listening for the voice of God.

Journaling my prayers gives me the opportunity to look back and see how God has answered them. As an example, His answer has often been revealed through an unrelated sermon the very next day. I learn new lessons from the Bible and meditate on how they impact me. I soak in the light of His Word as it reveals my sin. I confess it and allow Him to prune me. Mind you, I'm still juggling my family and their needs, but I'm able to spend more quality time with Jesus each day.

God gives me the most amazing revelations during my time away with Him in the summer. He uses that time to prepare me for what is to come. Without fail, what I learn over the summer is what I will need throughout the year. I spend a lot of time walking in the woods and on bike paths. I use this time to talk to Him. When we give Him time and space, He always responds.

One of my journal entries from 2014 reveals what the Lord spoke to me about during that time. He showed me that He was actually using my summers to get me away, to have me all to Himself and to strip me of myself. I had written, "He wants me to see that He is my Shepherd, that He will lead me, teach me, mentor me, and give me a word in due season. He wants to be my #1! He doesn't want me to rely on anyone else. He has made it evident that He doesn't want to share my affections or my needs, or be focused on anyone else but Him. When I think about it, that's actually when life works best."

He wants this for all of us. Can you find moments to give Him through your weeks and months to allow intimacy to grow? It's about being intentional as much as our time allows.

The only way to discover our true potential is to clear out the clutter and focus on what matters—the Lord Jesus Christ. Practicing biblical meditation will result in living a holy life.

Study to shew thyself approved unto God, a
workman that needeth not to be ashamed,
rightly dividing the word of truth.

2 Timothy 2:15 KJV

CHAPTER 7

ABIDING IN THE POWER OF THE HOLY SPIRIT THROUGH PRAYER, WORSHIP, AND FASTING

The Holy Spirit is the most crucial aspect of your relationship with the Father and Jesus. It saddens me that there is a lack of acknowledgment and understanding of His role in our lives today. Scriptures tell us that Jesus said He was leaving us the Holy Spirit for our benefit.

We cannot live the abundant life promised by God without the Holy Spirit. What would happen if you tried to bake a cake with one-third of the ingredients missing and only baked it two-thirds of the way? It would be a half-baked mess! We would never bake like that, so why would we live our lives like this? Living without the acknowledgment and involvement of the Holy Spirit in your life is like that half-baked cake.

Your power source is incomplete without the Holy Spirit.

When the Holy Spirit dwells in you, He is literally abiding with you. Abiding means to remain, continue, stay, dwell, reside, endure, remain steadfast or faithful, to keep.[13] Oh, what a glorious promise! He is ever with us.

Allow me to show you in Scripture where Jesus has appointed the role of the Holy Spirit in our lives. Please read the following verses out loud to yourself, slowly. Truly listen and meditate (think deeply) on them.

> "But if the Spirit of Him who raised Jesus from the dead dwells in you, He who raised Christ Jesus from the dead will also give life to your mortal bodies through His Spirit who dwells in you." (Romans 8:11)

> "But I tell you the truth, it is to your advantage that I go away; for if I do not go away, the Helper will not come to you; but if I go, I will send Him to you." (John 16:7)

> "I have many more things to say to you, but you cannot bear them now. But when He, the Spirit of truth, comes, He will guide you into all the truth; for He will not speak on His own initiative, but whatever He hears, He will speak; and He will disclose to you what is to come." (John 16:12,13)

> "If you love Me, you will keep My commandments. I will ask the Father, and He will give you another **Helper,** that He may be with you forever; that is the **Spirit of truth**, whom the world cannot receive, because it does not see Him or know Him, but you know Him because **He abides with you and will be in you.** "I will not leave you as orphans; I will come to you. After a little while the world will no longer see Me, but you will see Me; because I live, you will live also. **In that**

---

[13] abide. Dictionary.com. Dictionary.com Unabridged. Random House, Inc. http://www.dictionary.com/browse/abide (accessed: September 7, 2017).

day you will know that I am in My Father, and you in Me, and I in you.

"He who has My commandments and keeps them is the one who loves Me; and he who loves Me will be loved by My Father, and I will love him and will disclose Myself to him." Judas (not Iscariot) said to Him, "Lord, what then has happened that You are going to disclose Yourself to us and not to the world?" Jesus answered and said to him, "**If anyone loves Me, he will keep My word; and My Father will love him, and We will come to him and make Our abode with him.** He who does not love Me does not keep My words; and the word which you hear is not Mine, but the Father's who sent Me.

"These things I have spoken to you while abiding with you. **But the Helper, the Holy Spirit, whom the Father will send in My name, He will teach you all things, and bring to your remembrance all that I said to you.** Peace I leave with you; My peace I give to you; not as the world gives do I give to you. Do not let your heart be troubled, nor let it be fearful. You heard that I said to you, 'I go away, and I will come to you.' If you loved Me, you would have rejoiced because I go to the Father, for the Father is greater than I. Now I have told you before it happens, so that when it happens, you may believe. I will not speak much more with you, for the ruler of the world is coming, and he has nothing in Me; but so that the world may know that I love the Father, I do exactly as the Father commanded Me. Get up, let us go from here." (John 14:15-31, emphasis added)

Pause: Did God reveal the necessity of the Holy Spirit's involvement in your life through these portions of Scripture? Not acknowledging or understanding the Holy Spirit's presence, role, and function in your life is a spiritual trap. The consequence of falling into this trap is that you will lack His power and will be ineffective for the Kingdom of God.

Abiding brings the power of the presence of the Holy Spirit.

We are exhorted to abide and to rely on the Holy Spirit to help us navigate life. Meditating is a form of abiding. The evidence of our abiding is shown by how much fruit we bear. Jesus tells us in John 15:5-6, "Abide in Me, and I in you. As the branch cannot bear fruit of itself unless it abides in the vine, so neither can you unless you abide in Me. I am the vine, you are the branches; he who abides in Me and I in him, he bears much fruit, for apart from Me you can do nothing."

You have no need to worry. Your trust level should gradually increase as you pour out to the Lord in your quiet time. Meditation gives pause for you to position yourself to abide with the Holy Spirit. The more you see His faithfulness, the more you will desire of Him. The Holy Spirit's job is to guide us, direct us, and teach us. Jesus says He will teach us all things. Not some things, not a few things, but *all* things.

Too often, we rely on others to feed and teach us the ways of God. We try to justify our lifestyle rather than aligning our life with the Bible. God says, "I want to teach you." But if we're too busy, even busy doing good, we will miss a key principle in growing and developing our relationship with Jesus. That key principle is **abiding**.

Now remember, God is in us. We don't create the ambiance of His presence; His presence is ever with us. I love the phrase "soaking in God's presence." Soaking up time with Him, really enjoying being still and quiet, is a gift. It gives us an opportunity to hear from Him, read the Scriptures, and avoid interruptions so that the Holy Spirit can minister to our souls. Think of what the word *soak* means. It means an act of wetting something thoroughly; saturate; to penetrate or become known to the mind or feelings.[14] I want you to think about that.

After you soak in His presence, you should come out dripping Jesus! We press in and get filled up so we can pour out to others. This is a perfect example of the Scripture mentioned earlier, "I must decrease, and He must increase." So many of us pour out to other people. But in that pouring out, we can only give what we have. *It is essential to refuel and refill.* Refilling can only come from the main source, which is God. We always want to be in a place where we're giving from the overflow of Jesus. If we don't refill with God, we start to give from ourselves. That gets a little tricky and yucky.

How do we get that filling? By abiding and meditating in the Word. Be in the Word morning, noon, and night. Choose a verse and meditate on it all day. Memorize it. For example, you could read Proverbs 3:5, 6. "Trust in the Lord with all your heart, and lean not on your own understanding; In all your ways acknowledge Him, And He shall direct your paths."

Do we trust in the Lord as much as we trust in our cruise control? We set our vehicle to the speed we think is most productive. There are no breaks; the speed remains constant. Abiding is like turning off the highway of life at a rest stop. The rest stop offers us a break from that constant movement; it allows us to get out of the vehicle, stretch our legs, bend our backs, and sit quietly for a few moments to rest and regain momentum. Rest is an essential part of our lives. As born again believers, taking the time to abide in God is being intentional to get all the benefits of resting in Him.

I encourage you to memorize these verses:

Psalm 119:165 says, "Great peace have they which love thy law: and nothing shall offend them." Meditate on this. What does it mean? We are coming to understand His mercy, grace, and love. It's the perfect opportunity to journal what you see as you meditate on these verses.

---

[14] soak. Dictionary.com. *Dictionary.com Unabridged.* Random House, Inc. http://www.dictionary.com/browse/soak (accessed: September 7, 2017).

"Blessed are those who hunger and thirst for righteousness, for they shall be satisfied." (Matthew 5:6) Remember that filling I was telling you about? "And to know the love of Christ which passes knowledge; that you may be filled with all the fullness of God." (Ephesians 3:19 NKJV) Filling is so important. Scripture says, "Be not drunk with wine, wherein is excess; but be filled with the Spirit." (Ephesians 5:18)

You are indwelt by the Holy Spirit if you are born again. *The Holy Spirit takes up residence in you.* However, sometimes the flesh rears its ugly head. What He's saying here is to make sure you're flowing from the Spirit. He says, "For this cause, we also, since the day we heard it, do not cease to pray for you and to desire that you might be filled with the knowledge of His will in all wisdom and spiritual understanding." (Colossians 1:9)

Prayer

When we think of abiding, prayer and worship are the most common ways to draw closer to the Lord, to build that bond, to meditate on Him, and to be in His presence.

Prayer is coming before the Lord, presenting our petitions, and offering praise and honor to our God. It should be our constant communion with God. Each of us should be in prayer as much as possible throughout the day. That is practicing the presence of God.

The privilege to pray, whether alone or with the Body of Christ, is a gift. When like-minded people come together and pray, watch out! The ground begins to shake. God hears and answers. He is delighted to acknowledge all of our prayers, whether it's your first time praying or you are a seasoned prayer warrior. He loves it all!

You may ask, what does prayer really look like? It's a personal interaction. Prayer is our means of communion with God, a way to express praise and adoration to Him. Prayer is often mixed with reciting God's Word back to Him, along with sharing those things that are heavy on our hearts. We pray because we desire to see God move on our behalf. However, regardless of what we petition, our ultimate desire should be "Thy will be done," not "my will be done." Prayer is our primary means of seeing God work in the lives of others. Prayer allows us to plug into His power. Prayer is our weapon in overcoming the enemy and his traps. James 5:16 tells us that the fervent prayer of a righteous man accomplishes much.

The Lord's Prayer, found in Matthew 6:9-13, reveals an example of how our hearts should be postured as we pray. Psalm 100:4,5 shows what the attitude of our hearts should look like as we come before Him: "Enter into His gates with thanksgiving, and into His courts with praise: be thankful unto Him, and bless His name." The Lord wants your sincere heart, your praise, and your adoration. He is so faithful to listen to all of your needs and concerns. However, it has to be more than just a long laundry list of requests. That would be a one-sided relationship, making it all about us.

Worship

Ahhhh, worship is more than a song. It's a lifestyle. Worship is a heart attitude. It is expressing reverence and adoration for a deity.

Praise Him! Read 1 Chronicles 16:23-31 aloud:

> "Sing to the LORD, all the earth; proclaim His salvation day after day. Declare His glory among the nations, His marvelous deeds among all peoples. For great is the LORD and most worthy of praise; He is to be feared above all God's. For all the God's of the nations are idols, but the LORD made the heavens. Splendor and majesty are before Him; strength and joy are in His dwelling place. Ascribe to the LORD, all you families of nations, ascribe to the LORD glory and strength. Ascribe to the LORD the glory due His name; bring an offering and come before Him. Worship the LORD in the splendor of His holiness. Tremble before Him, all the earth! The world is firmly established; it cannot be moved. Let the heavens rejoice, let the earth be glad; let them say among the nations, "The LORD reigns!""

When we worship God, we humble ourselves and lift Him up. We bring praise, thanksgiving, adoration, and honor to our King. We position our hearts in submission to His authority and our lifestyle reflects *His* song. Worship is the release of great joy as we enter into His presence with thanksgiving in our hearts.

> **Worship is an expression of the heart.**
> **Worship shifts the atmosphere.**
> **Worship is our weapon in battling unseen spiritual warfare.**
> **Worship ushers in the presence of God.**
> **Worship is powerful!**

Check out this special circumstance recorded in the Bible. Jehoshaphat sent the singers out to battle first before the army. God told them to go into battle with their praises as their front line advantage. Think on that for a while. God asked them to trust Him because this was His battle. How often do we take on God's battles and react by going in with guns blazing? Worship was the answer here. When we are faced with difficulty, this is a good reminder to ask God what He wants of us before assuming that the common response is best.

> "And they rose early in the morning, and went forth into the wilderness of Tekoa: and as they went forth, Jehoshaphat stood and said, Hear me, O Judah, and ye inhabitants of Jerusalem; Believe in the Lord your God, so shall ye be established; believe His prophets, so shall ye prosper. And when he had consulted with the people, he appointed singers unto the Lord, and that should praise the beauty of holiness, as they went out before the army, and to say, Praise the Lord; for His mercy endureth for ever. And when they began to sing and to praise, the Lord set ambushments against the children of Ammon, Moab, and mount Seir, which were come against Judah; and they were smitten." (2 Chronicles 20:20-22)

Wow! Will you have the courage to praise God in your darkest hours? In your scariest trials? When you feel like all odds are against you? Will you trust Him for your outcome?

Practice makes perfect. I cannot express enough the importance of being proactive in having your own worship sessions in the privacy of your own home. When worship becomes part of your lifestyle, it will be your first response when hard times come.

Private worship sessions are incredible and certainly create a lifestyle change of pressing in and seeking His holiness. I love to soak in His presence, lift up His praises and sing of His goodness and love. It lifts my spirit and gives me an internal joy. Oh, how I adore spending time with Him and praising His Holy name. It's a pleasure!

Worship is a feeling or expression of reverence and adoration for God. How do you worship Him?

Biblical Fasting

Fasting is another form of meditation. It is one of the most serious of all meditation practices. Obedience in fasting has brought me healing, clarity, and answers.

When should we fast? Jesus says, "*When* you fast." Not if. *When.* It is expected. This is another "necessity, not an option" principle. Jesus fasted. Fasting is when you are led by the Holy Spirit to press in, you are desperate for Him, or you desire to draw closer. The more you meditate and draw closer to God, the more you may desire to make this practice a routine in your lifestyle. If you are unable to fast due to health reasons, ask for others to fast on your behalf. Queen Esther called a community fast. Believing you don't need to fast when you are physically and medically able is a spiritual trap.

I feel obligated to share this important disclaimer: This information concerns health and medical conditions and should not be taken as advice, nor treated as such. Do not rely on the information in this book, but consult your healthcare provider.

A true biblical fast is abstaining from food.

This exhortation is for those who are physically and medically able to biblically fast. Fasting is an intentional choice to press in and obey God. A typical fast is generally from breakfast to breakfast. Notice that breakfast is actually "breaking the fast." However, many people fast on different 24-hour schedules.

It is not easy to fast, period. In the Scriptures, there are a few different lengths of time that people fasted. They fasted twenty-four hours, three days, seven days, forty days. David says he afflicted himself with fasting. Fasting sobers us up to reality and our desperate need for Jesus. Let's establish what the Scriptures tell us that fasting means:

In the Strong's Concordance[15], fasting in Hebrew means: abstain from food, fast, primitive root to cover over the mouth, that is to fast; To abstain from food; in Greek: abstinence from food.

Matthew 4:4 tells us that man shall not live on bread alone, but on every word that proceeds out of the mouth of God. There is a reason God chose food as His fast. Food sustains us. If we rely on food rather than God, we won't experience His strength in our weakness. When we surrender ourselves in humility and obedience by giving up our physical sustenance and relying completely on His spiritual power, we are trusting Him completely. Also, food dictates what we do. Our lives are surrounded by our meals. We live to eat.

Fasting is one more form of us slowing down and being still. However, *in slowing down through fasting, we will find our breakthroughs that propel us forward.* Fasting is another way to give up what we think is good so God can give us more.

I love the story of the little girl who had the sweetest imitation pearl necklace. One day, her daddy came home and said, "I have something for you. But in order for me to give this to you, I need you to give me your pearl necklace in exchange." She just loved her pearls. She tightly clenched what she thought was the most valuable thing in the world. She didn't understand they weren't real. Imitation or not, they were

---

[15] Strong, James. 1890. Strong's exhaustive concordance of the Bible. Abingdon Press.

the best she thought she would ever have. Meanwhile, her daddy held a set of beautiful, authentic pearls behind his back. Her little hands couldn't hold both sets. So, like a good father, he asked her to release what she held in her hands so he could replace it with something more, something better.

How can we apply this little story to our own lives? Are you holding onto spiritual traps, thinking they are good? Daddy has more for you— authentic relationships, authentic drawing closer, authentic truth. The things we clutch the most can become spiritual traps that hold us back from intimacy with our Father. What holds you back?

I believe the need for control and clutching what we think belongs to us is a struggle for all of us. But I think this little story helps us see that when we release anything and everything God asks us to, He's a good, good Daddy. He's going to give us something better. I hope this encourages you moving forward to see that, whatever you may have to give up to get this time alone with Him, He's going to give you something better. Stay focused on wanting more from Him. Understand that with this investment, just like anything else, whatever you put in will determine the yield of your return. This is the principle of "what you sow, you will reap." This will be the greatest return on anything you could invest in throughout your life. It will literally change your life. You can't afford to live without more of God.

Here is what a 24-hour fast looks like for me:

Once I commit, I'm a stickler. There is no cheating. If I accidentally put something in my mouth, I reset the clock. God knows and sees all; I am going to commit with integrity. I do drink water. It's important for you to drink half your body weight in ounces of water every day. If you fast, you should make sure you fulfill that requirement.

During my fast, I spend time talking to God about the concerns that led me to fast. Oftentimes the Lord will put something on my heart to pray for while I am fasting and I will add that to my initial reason for fasting. I spend time reading my Bible. Sometimes I just sit and meditate on Him. I intertwine this with my regular activities. However, if I fast for a longer period of time, I try to release myself from my daily routine. I have found that this works best for me physically. If my belly growls, I tell it "man shall not live by bread alone" (I kid you not). It reminds me to keep going even when it's uncomfortable.

Here is just one testimony of how fasting empowers us and brings breakthroughs:

One day, the Lord put it on my heart to fast and pray for a few people. My girlfriend's daughter was one of them. I sensed there was a need, but had no idea of what that need was. I emailed my friend and let her know I was fasting for her.

After my fast, the Lord revealed some things about her situation that I felt were too difficult to share. I actually decided I didn't want to confront her with these things. A week later, my girlfriend came up to me and asked, "Can I talk with you?" Gotta love it when the Lord sets you up! I asked if she received the email I sent. She said, "No, I haven't been on the computer."

My friend told me she wanted to talk to me about some things her daughter was struggling with. I instantly told her that God had prompted me to fast for her, and that I had not been obedient to share what the Lord showed me. After I asked for and received her forgiveness, I began to tell her what He revealed to me. She stopped me. "My girlfriend at work told me the exact same thing you're saying, word for word, just two days ago!"

I learned a very important lesson in this. We're often too embarrassed or fearful to obey what God tells us. He certainly redeemed me even in my stubbornness, but I missed the blessing I would have received if I had gone to her when He told me to. Also notice that the Lord prompted me to fast for her without giving me a reason. He gave me insight to share and was gracious even in my delay to meet her need through someone else. Do you see just how much God loves us? He is sovereign; the job will get done with or without us. What a gift to be invited into His work. What a pleasure to have a front row seat to see how He works it all out!

Fasting brings our bodies under subjection to God. It teaches us discipline.

We can be motivated by our stomachs. Have you ever noticed that you can become very cranky, irritable, and unreasonable when you're hungry? People will do almost anything for food. Genesis 25:29-34 tells us that Esau sold his birthright for a bowl of stew. Proverbs 28:21 says that a man will sin for a piece of bread.

When we put fasting into practice, we enter into training to yield to God rather than giving over to the cry of our hunger pains. Feeling and hearing an empty stomach can give us pause. It certainly puts into perspective how blessed we are to eat and be filled. There are many people in the world who don't have the luxury of eating three meals a day. Some are fortunate to have three meals a week. Going without can help us focus on the needs of others.

Fasting can bring God's favor in a crisis

When Mordecai informed Esther of Haman's decree to kill all the Jews, she implored all the Jews in Susa to fast with her for three days and three nights.

> "In each and every province where the command and decree of the king came, there was great mourning among the Jews, with fasting, weeping and wailing; and many lay on sackcloth and ashes." (Esther 4:3)

> "Go, assemble all the Jews who are found in Susa, and fast for me; do not eat or drink for three days, night or day. I and my maidens also will fast in the same way. And thus I will go in to the king, which is not according to the law; and if I perish, I perish." (Esther 4:16)

> In short, favor came when Esther went in before the king. The king declared another decree giving the Jews permission to defend themselves.

Fasting rejuvenates the body

Fasting is a spiritual discipline that yields spiritual and physical results. So much so, that in our obedience spiritually God heals our bodies physically. In 24 hours, our bodies take time to heal—a break from digesting food. It's a double blessing.

Fasting from material things such as cell phones, TV, Facebook, etc., is an exercise that tears down potential idols. Anything that has power over you is an idol. A great discipline to overcome idols is to eliminate them from your life. You might be led to fast from one of these things for a period of time in order to release its hold over you.

Fasting breaks the bonds of wickedness

Fasting can bring deliverance for ourselves and others. I encourage you to read Isaiah 58. Please take note of the type of fast that is pleasing to God and what type of fast is unacceptable to Him. This is too good to pass up. Use this time to meditate on the chapter. What did the Lord show you?

Fasting is expected of us. Fasting is good for us. God knows what we need before we need it. So many benefits come out of our obedience. *Fasting is a gift.* Ask God to reveal what He desires of you personally. No one should tell you that you must fast. God is adamant that we fast for the right reasons. *He will help you discover what is best for you.* I can only encourage you and share what it has done for me. But notice, God knows what we need. Even when we don't get what we want, we can claim Romans 8:28, "God causes all things to work together for good" *if we are yielded and surrendered to His perfect will and accept His answer.* **Watch out for the spiritual traps that may keep you from experiencing His power in fasting.**

There are times and seasons where it seems God has not answered our prayers and fasting. For example, you may pray for a struggling marriage, a wayward child, or someone who needs healing. Don't stop if you don't receive an immediate answer.

A testimonony of God's faithfulness to me through the years

Just so you know, this did not come overnight. God's answers came through my obedience to persistently take these things to the throne of grace, petitioning God for answers. Sometimes we have to wait, but we should never give up. Giving up is not an option!

I asked for forgiveness . . . He forgave me.

I prayed and fasted for a godly man . . .
He sent me my soul mate.

I fasted for guidance . . . He led my way.

I prayed for my children . . . one by one He opened the womb.

I fasted for wisdom . . . He enabled me.

I fasted for discernment . . . He opened my eyes.

I fasted for freedom . . . He set me free.

I fasted for my marriage . . . He changed me.

I fasted for the spiritual health of my family . . . He had me homeschooling.

I fasted for my child's health . . . a miracle.

I fasted and prayed for yet another child's frailty . . . another miracle!

I prayed for clarity . . . He cleared my mind.

I fasted for ministry . . . He opened doors.

I fasted for help . . . He built a team.

I fasted for unity . . . He poured out His Holy Spirit.

I fasted for others . . . He gave me revelation, insights, and open doors.

I fasted for understanding . . . He made me rest.

I fasted for a pure heart . . . He cleansed me.

I fasted for kindred spirits . . . He blessed me.

I fasted for truth to be known . . . He revealed hearts and motives.

I fasted for a hunger and thirst for Him . . .
He fills me to the overflow.

I fasted for chains to break . . . He broke them.

I fasted to love Him with my whole heart . . . He drew me.

I fasted for a calling . . . He compelled me.

I fasted for the salvation of others . . . He saved to the uttermost.

I fasted for reconciliation . . . He restored.

I fasted for healing for my husband . . . He renewed.

I offer myself as a living sacrifice . . . to
my amazement He uses me.

I could go on and on and on. Jesus never fails. Great things He
has done! **He has been faithful in my lifetime, to God be the glory!**

*If you abide in Me, and My words abide in you, ask
whatever you wish, and it will be done for you.*

John 15:7

CHAPTER 8

HOW MEDITATION CHANGED MY LIFE

Reflecting back on the premature birth of my son, it changed me for the better forever. God showed up for me in a big way that first night at the hospital. I was in recovery for over eight hours after delivering my son. They had wheeled him to my bedside in a box called an isolette at about 6:00 pm. I thought it was like a warming box. He didn't seem to be in distress. The visit only lasted a few seconds before they wheeled him away. This whole experience felt unreal; I felt like a character in a movie who had just given birth, and the baby was whisked away quickly.

I didn't see him until nine hours later. As my husband was getting ready to leave, I asked him to take me to the NICU in a wheelchair. I had to see my baby boy! It was killing me. He wheeled me down and then I had to wash up and put scrubs on. I thought to myself, *this is interesting.* I had no idea what I was about to enter into. When you're in the hospital, you don't get to see the NICU with windows. This area is hidden, quarantined from most people.

Everything my eyes took in was overwhelming. So many moms and dads huddled around clear plastic boxes that held their precious little ones. Beeps, sirens, bells, and whistles were going off randomly all over the ward. Wires, monitors, emergency care—where in the world was I?

We arrived at my baby boy's isolette. I gasped, my jaw dropped, and I thought, *I'm in a nightmare! Wake me up!* He was so tiny, only 2.5 pounds. He had wires connected to him everywhere. Monitors and emergency care units were set in place. I took a deep breath and prayed, "Lord, hold me up! Don't let me cry, my baby boy needs to hear my voice. I need to be strong." Even now, I cannot put into words how this experience struck me. Honestly, I was ignorant to this corner of the world where preemies were cared for.

I spoke through the hole in the box, calling his name and whispering sweet nothings. He turned his little head toward the opening and tried to open his eye to see me. I lost it! I wanted to hold him, kiss him, tell him it was going to be okay, Mommy was here. I wasn't allowed to touch his skin; it was super sensitive being outside the womb 11 weeks early. I felt such a range of emotions; I'm still not sure how I held it together.

The nurses suggested that I go back to my room and rest because I was very weak. My hubby was ready to go home to our other three children. All I could think about was that my baby was by himself, he was very sick, and I wasn't the one caring for him. I was out of my mind!

My hubby tucked me into my hospital bed, prayed with me, kissed me and said goodnight, and off he went. I sat in bed, completely stunned. I stared blankly at the wall. I started to cry. Nothing was as I thought it should be. My whole life had just come to a halt. I was all by myself, separated from my infant, and feeling extremely alone. We had left the house abruptly to get to the hospital when my water broke, so I didn't have time to grab my Bible.

I began to cry and sob, and then I went into the ugly cry. No noises. Just plain hysterical crying with no air, no sound. The Holy Spirit nudged me to reach over to the nightstand and open the top drawer to see if there was a Gideon Bible. Yes, there was. I was relieved. I desperately asked, "Lord, I need you. Help me."

I flipped the Bible open to John 14. Verse 1 says, "Do not let your heart be troubled; believe in God, believe also in me." I lost it! Let my heart not be troubled. I was so troubled! God made Himself very real to me that night in that hospital room. Yes, I believe, Lord! Yes, I believe!

He revealed Himself to me through His Word. He made it evident that He wanted to calm me down and give me His peace. He got my attention. I prayed and communed with God until I fell asleep.

God began retraining me

From that day forward I had to ask myself, *am I going to keep relying on myself, or will I rely on the Lord?* Remember how busy I was? This came with no warning. I was entering into a new chapter of my life. A new season. The hardest part was giving up control. I did not want anyone else caring for my son. I didn't want to leave him there and go home. And I didn't want to be in that hospital for 10 hours a day. Guess what, it didn't matter what I wanted anymore. God was calling the shots.

I was overwhelmed for many reasons. I had three precious babies at home without their momma; I was scheduled to speak at a retreat that weekend (remember my son wasn't expected to arrive for almost three more months); I was facilitating a weekly video Bible study, which the women were just beginning to enjoy. Who would care for them? Who would take over for me? I kept thinking of everything I would miss out on. How would the world go on without me? Well, like it or not, life does go on without us.

I started praying about everything. *God's peace sheltered me in the moment.* It grew over time. As I came to see the benefits of meditating on the Lord, I developed a need for more and more. I learned to renew my mind by replacing old thoughts with God's promises. I was a work in progress. I thank God every day for not giving up on me. I am such a hard head.

I did not want to make one decision about my son without the Lord. I constantly asked Him for wisdom, guidance, and understanding. I asked for His will to be done, not mine. Not only had I found the secret to a closer walk with God, my longing for "something more" was finally fulfilled. He gave me God-stories with every move. He continues to show up and show off in my life as I press in.

Philippians 4:6,7 reminds us, "Be anxious for nothing, but in everything by prayer and supplication with thanksgiving let your requests be made known to God. And the peace of God, which surpasses all comprehension, will guard your hearts and your minds in Christ Jesus."

I memorized this verse and meditated on it constantly. It went against my nature to surrender myself to it. I struggled and resisted so much in the beginning. But once I finally let go and relaxed, I started to see so much more value and benefit. I have to say, my life has never been better. Me and my Daddy, Jesus my redeemer and bridegroom, and my helper the Holy Spirit are very tight to this day. My life changed drastically. I am not the same person I was six months ago, let alone a decade ago. I am forever grateful.

As I mentioned earlier, I was on bed rest right before my water broke. I had already begun pressing in and spending more quality time with the Lord. I believe that because I was being still and petitioning Him then, He was preparing and protecting me. When my water broke, they said that if we had not taken it so seriously and gotten to the hospital as quickly as we did, my baby and I both would have died. I was hemorrhaging and didn't even know it! God spared us both that day. He spared me from death, and He spared me from myself. *My whole experience was a training, a regrouping, an unlearning, an attention getter. He got my attention, all right. Meditation changed me, and it has changed the way I live my life.*

Benefits of meditation

One might ask, why should a born again believer meditate? Here are some benefits that I have discovered:

Enjoying the tranquility of being still and silent

I try to rid myself of noise pollution and enjoy the silence. We don't realize how much our brains take in from all five senses at once. There are way too many noises. I was blessed to discover this reality when I went to South Africa. After going on a safari, we had a Bible study with the workers that took care of the grounds and animals. Leaving at about 9:30 in the evening, we walked outside. Oh my, what a surprise. The moon and stars were the only light, dancing off the savanna. Everything else was completely dark. There was no light pollution from any man-made source. It was incredible. There were only natural sounds of the animals of the savanna calling to one another in the distance, bugs singing, and periods of almost complete silence. There were no planes flying overhead. I didn't hear a motor vehicle or any other kind of machinery or electrical unit—zero noise pollution. I experienced a gift from God that night. Silence is a gift!

Being set free

Pressing in and seeking God will save us from so much unnecessary negative energy that comes with spiritual traps. Those emotions waste a lot of time. They pull us down and make us feel yucky. When I catch my mind running, worrying, or being anxious, angry, or unforgiving, I go to a quiet place, sit, and pray. I take three deep breaths and exhale just to relieve the stress build up and decompress from whatever is bothering me. I claim God's promises by speaking them out loud. *I am met by His presence and He stabilizes me in His truth.* He meets me every time. I have come to expect this when I obey, taking the time to renew my mind and get my head straight. Being set free from sin, strongholds, and tormentors is more than enough motivation to sit at Jesus' feet.

One of the reasons Jesus came was to empower us to be set free from these tormentors. *Freedom begins when you go into your secret place, prayer closet, quiet place—whatever you want to call it—and press in to spend time alone with the Father.* Fear falls off, worry dissipates, and anxiety is replaced by peace. When we trust God, we find ourselves in the center of His presence. Do you see the benefit?

Resting from Busyness

Rest is the calling of Psalm 23. He leads us to still waters; He makes us lie down in green pastures. Slow down, enjoy life, stop to smell the roses. When we allow God to be a part of every area of our lives, there is a shift in how we respond to our busyness. We are much more centered on Him.

Finding peace

I don't know if your house is like mine. Every now and then it can get a little stressful. Managing everyone's lives, helping them with various tasks, caring for them long distance, listening to them battle. . .who's happy, who isn't happy, who knows what's best for so and so, and I am to blame for whatever doesn't look perfect! I don't yell "Calgon!" anymore, I run to Jesus. I go into my secret place and shut the door. I believe the Lord tells us to shut the door because He wants us to close off the world so we can rest and center ourselves in His peace.

Experiencing peace, comfort, and understanding

Several years ago, my husband was in a serious accident. A tree limb fell and hit him on the head. Working through the doctor reports, riding from one hospital to another, and getting him into the ER was so fast paced, I just couldn't catch my breath (an easy setup for a spiritual trap). I hadn't had time to pray or get my thoughts straight. I needed quiet, alone time with my Jesus so I asked a nurse if there was a private room I could use in order to get my balance in all of this. She led me to a little room. I went in, shut the door, and fell to my knees. I went right into fasting and prayer, surrendering everything for my husband's benefit and for God's perfect will to be done.

In my moment of silence, I heard Him say loud and clear in my mind, "This is not unto death, but unto transformation." I received instant peace for my worried, anxious mind. I got up off my knees, stood square, held my head high, and walked out of that room with complete trust—Daddy's got this. My husband didn't look good at all physically, but as illogical as it may have seemed, I had a peace and calmness to trust in what God told me. We really do need to trust in Him for everything. Unless you are in the habit of practicing meditation, this is easier said than done. Wasting too much time and energy on the unknown is a spiritual trap.

Gaining a better night's sleep

When I spend time with the Father before bed in prayer, worship, reading, and lifting up my voice in praise, I let out a sigh of release. After I have been in His presence, I experience a relaxation that feels like I'm floating on a big, white, fluffy cloud. My mind is already set on Him and I have no problem drifting off to sleep.

Learning to trust Him

When we're busy, we can be very protective of what little time we have. When I take the time to be still instead of allowing my day to dictate my steps, God redeems my time. He shows up and shows off! I speak out loud to my Daddy. I hear myself ramble my problems and complaints to Him. I find my resolution comes much faster when I say it out loud than when it stays stuck inside my head. He is so faithful to put up with me.

Pausing life to hear from Holy Spirit

You may ask, "How do you hear from God?" It isn't audible. For me personally, it's in my mind, or deep within my chest. It's usually something I wouldn't tell myself at first. It leaves me saying, "Yes. Lord. You are so right! Why didn't I think of that? I love it!" I love communing with God. He speaks to me through His Word as well. I take time to jot down what I hear from Him. It is just that important.

Receiving love and encouragement

When I'm struggling, I will turn to my Bible. Sometimes I may choose a portion of Scripture that I know is exactly what I need. Other times I will flip open and the page I land on will have the exact verse needed to convict me, comfort me, encourage me, instruct me, or express God's love for me. This is very special to me. I go into a quiet place. I envision myself curling up on my heavenly Daddy's lap. I picture Him loving on me and counseling me in secret, helping me to see His will in my situation. I am sold out and fully persuaded that He wants this for all of His kids! Meditation is key. When we struggle, we should run to Daddy, not to anyone else. Go to Him first. He never fails us!

Pause: Self-awareness equals God-awareness because God is in us! Self-discovery is important for personal growth. Be intentional about investing time in yourself for personal growth.

Learning about both God and yourself is vital for growing closer to Him. I believe it is important to study yourself. I have learned so much about myself through meditation. Transformation begins with a new level of awareness. The Holy Spirit helps you understand what moves you and what causes you pain. He reveals areas that need to be pruned away. Some might call this an inner intuition, but truthfully it's learning how to listen and receive from the Holy Spirit.

God-spirations

This is where the Lord wows me with His encouragement. He inspires me through His Word on so many levels. Meditating on the Word and pressing in inspires me to be more, to live life to the fullest in Christ Jesus.

Inner peace

Meditation will help you find the inner peace most people seek. That inner peace comes from the Lord Jesus Christ. As we focus our minds on His holiness and righteousness, then His love will bring us to a new level in our relationship with Himself and others. Just think how pleasant our interactions would be if we were all centered on Christ.

Change in attitude

When you spend time with the Holy Spirit, you will exhibit the fruit of the Spirit: love, joy, peace, patience, kindness, goodness, faithfulness, gentleness, and self-control. You will respond from what you have been building up. Drawing closer to God develops a sensitivity to be led by the Spirt instead of yourself. Pride and flesh are put in their places. They become less and less a part of you.

There are so many more benefits. I am just naming some that have impacted me. The more you practice the principle of meditation, the more benefits you will discover for yourself as well.

Here is a key concept that you don't want to miss. Every believer needs to understand the difference between conviction and condemnation. "Beloved, do not believe every spirit, but test the spirits to see whether they are from God, because many false prophets have gone out into the world." (1 John 4:1) I heard a sermon once where the preacher said, "Condemnation drives you from God, while conviction draws you to God."

Condemnation is most definitely a spiritual trap. The enemy says, "Look what you did! You're despicable. You'll never amount to anything. You make this mistake all the time. You might as well go run and hide under a rock." *That's not God!* Anything that brings condemning guilt and shame is not of God, it's from the pit of hell. *It's important to understand the difference between how God deals with us and how the enemy seeks to destroy us.*

The enemy uses lies to hold us in a place of contempt. Those lies become our thoughts. *Those thoughts are just thoughts. We have the power to tear those thoughts down by believing the promises God has given us in His Word.*

Condemnation brings in guilt and shame; we feel bad and remain isolated and stuck. We may even cry as we acknowledge our part because of sin. But our pride keeps us far from God. The enemy works overtime to keep us from accepting His forgiveness and we wear the weight of the world on our shoulders.

Conviction comes from the Holy Spirit bringing an awareness that we are in sin, yet comforting us with the knowledge that we can take it to the Lord and be forgiven. It hurts us to hurt Jesus. We take Him at His Word and trust Him that we can freely move forward after acknowledging our sin. We sense a loving hand or a word of correction that excites us to get up and try again. All we have to do is believe it, be fully persuaded that we are forgiven, and get back in the game for the Kingdom of God.

Consequences of neglecting meditation

What might the consequences be if you don't spend time with God? What if you don't press in, don't take time out for Him, don't slow down and be still? *When you don't practice meditation it puts you in a spiritual trap of complacency, in spiritual bondage, or remaining trapped in negativity.* You can also struggle with being calm, level headed, and Spirit-led. When you spend time with God in stillness, it gives Him the opportunity to speak truth over you and to counteract the lies of the enemy. Don't let your adversary hold you down!

I remember one particular time a conflict arose. I didn't understand what was going on. My head and heart hurt, I was sick to my stomach, I was confused and overwhelmed. Have you been there? I tried to "fix" it. I approached the parties in my "chaotic state" of nervousness and it did not, I repeat, it did not go over well. I was not in control of my emotions at all.

If I had known the importance of pressing in with God before putting myself out there to try to rectify this conflict, I would have been more relaxed. The Lord might have given me wisdom and instructions on how to handle it. I could have asked Him if He even wanted me to try to rectify this conflict. Instead, I was not Spirit-led. I lacked wisdom. I admit it. It was that bad. My mind was on overload with thoughts and concerns, and my soul lacked stillness. Because I had not pressed in with God, I was unable to steady myself in truth and peace. That's what a spiritual trap looks like in real time.

Here are a few consequences of not meditating: we may miss unknown opportunities, we may miss out on the peace we desperately need, and we may miss the answers we are searching for. Most of all, we may miss out on the substance of a healthy relationship with our God. **A relationship that is not nurtured and maintained will lack so much of what is needed that it will barely survive.** We can relate this to our human relationships. We must be intentional to invest and be proactive in our relationships. I am determined to truly seek my Daddy's wisdom and rest in a situation before moving out. I have learned valuable lessons. Unless He prompts me to move, I prefer to just sit. I have learned the power in waiting on Him and can testify that He always takes care of what we need when we need it.

Do we even realize how busy our days can be as we rush around? We can be overwhelmed. We really need to have a built-in appointment every day to sit still, be silent, and receive what He may have for us. In doing so, we will stabilize ourselves in His peace and presence so that we may respond to others from the fruit of the Spirit, rather than from our sinful selves. I reiterate this so much so that it will be embedded in your thoughts.

Now we know Matthew 6:33 says, "Seek ye first the kingdom of God and his righteousness." (KJV) That's really what meditation is—if done the right way. It's seeking *His* righteousness. It's pondering on it. It's offering up something you may be struggling with. It's pondering on the Scriptures. It's an opportunity to really spend time with Him. *But it is certainly not to manipulate reality. Biblical meditation is not about emptying your mind and letting it be filled with the unknown.* It doesn't create an ambience for you to gain "brownie points" with God. That's not what this is about. It's really not about anything other than building an intimate relationship with Him. When we don't press in, we can lack so much: hearing His voice, finding His peace, unloading our worries, being still and at rest. . .the list goes on and it describes the spiritual trap we can find ourselves in.

We cannot manufacture our desired outcome. We must give up control, trust God with the results, and rest in His peace and presence as we wait on Him and be still. There is a difference. Meditation is only for spiritual purposes; we cannot think of it as an opportunity to get us what we want in life.

Our busy lifestyles create a greater need for meditation. As busy as our lives have become, we should be running to our quiet place of being still in order to ponder and reflect on our God more and more. Desperation for the Lord should override every other pleasure. Meditation gives us pause in our day to really pay attention, to see what He wants to say to us or how He wants to lead us. *He is always with us. However, we are not always in His presence.* **When busyness overtakes "presence," we become overwhelmed by the present or the immediate.** There's a huge difference. Can you see that?

My life has never been the same since the Lord taught me the importance of meditation. He taught me that I needed to slow down. I needed to repent of my busyness and turn towards Jesus.

It's important to understand that meditation is so much more than just reading the Bible. It's about digging deeper, contemplating, giving God room to speak to you through His Word. Bible study allows us to gain knowledge and understanding for application. As we meditate, we connect with God through that knowledge and understanding. This deepens our intimacy with God and raises our awareness of how much more of a loving, holy God He really is.

Looking back, it's hard to imagine a time when I didn't understand the meaning of meditation or take it seriously. Praise God, I've learned to identify the spiritual traps. Boy, I didn't know what I was missing out on. It wasn't until I looked into it for myself that I started on a new journey in drawing closer to God. The more I read my Bible intent on finding answers, the more it pointed to what was needed. I learned meditation from the Holy Spirit as I was seeking more of God. That is where I discovered the richness and depth to my time with God, who I now call Daddy.

As our time comes to a close, I offer a prayer for you, my new friend. Thank you for walking out a bit of my journey with me.

> Daddy, I pray for my new friend. You know their name, You know how many hairs are on their head, You created them for Your glory. I ask in Jesus' name for You to encourage them. Inspire them for more of Yourself. Draw them close. Help them to pause from their busy life, to slow down, to be still, and meet You in an intimate way. I ask that they will be able to hear Your whisper. That they sense Your protection and love all

around them. That the more they practice walking in Your presence, the more they come to find Your richness in glory, righteousness, and faithfulness.

May the Holy Spirit guide, direct, teach, and reveal the greater truths from Scriptures that will set my friend free. I pray that my personal experience inspires them to want more for themselves. That they realize You are always with them and it is always better to walk life out together with Jesus. Father, show up and show off for my new friend. Give them a new zeal to love and seek after You. May they come to treasure You more today than yesterday. In Jesus' name I pray. Thank You Holy Spirit in advance for blessing my new friend and giving them favor beyond measure in their relationship with You! Amen

Because this guide is all about coming to know God more intimately through reading, meditating, and memorizing Scripture with the intent that it will change your life, I pray the Scripture below for you as well. I ask that you pray this over yourself. Meditate on the richness of what it is saying to you. Take it in, live it out. Own it as yours!

With so much love for the brethren,
Your friend, Debbie

The Blessings of Redemption (Ephesians chapter 1 NASB)

Paul, an apostle of Christ Jesus by the will of God, to the saints who are at Ephesus and who are faithful in Christ Jesus: Grace to you and peace from God our Father and the Lord Jesus Christ. Blessed be the God and Father of our Lord Jesus Christ, who has blessed us with every spiritual blessing in the heavenly places in Christ, just as He chose us in Him before the foundation of the world, that we would be holy and blameless before Him. In love He predestined us to adoption as sons through Jesus Christ to Himself, according to the kind intention of His will, to the praise of the glory of His grace, which He freely bestowed on us in the Beloved.

In Him we have redemption through His blood, the forgiveness of our trespasses, according to the riches of His grace which He lavished on us. In all wisdom and insight He made known to us the mystery of His will, according to His kind intention which He purposed in Him with a view to an administration suitable to the fullness of the times, that is, the summing up of all things in Christ, things in the heavens and things on the earth.

In Him also we have obtained an inheritance, having been predestined according to His purpose who works all things after the counsel of His will, to the end that we who were the first to hope in Christ would be to the praise of His glory. In Him, you also, after listening to the message of truth, the gospel of your salvation— having also believed, you were sealed in Him with the Holy Spirit of promise, who is given as a pledge of our inheritance, with a view to the redemption of God's own possession, to the praise of His glory.

For this reason I too, having heard of the faith in the Lord Jesus which exists among you and your love for all the saints, do not cease giving thanks for you, while making mention of you in my prayers; that the God of our Lord Jesus Christ, the Father of glory, may give to you a spirit of wisdom and of revelation in the knowledge of Him.

I pray that the eyes of your heart may be enlightened, so that you will know what is the hope of His calling, what are the riches of the glory of His inheritance in the saints, and what is the surpassing greatness of His power toward us who believe. These are in accordance with the working of the strength of His might which He brought about in Christ, when He raised Him from the dead and seated Him at His right hand in the heavenly places, far above all rule and authority and power and dominion, and every name that is named, not only in this age but also in the one to come. And He put all things in subjection under His feet, and gave Him as head over all things to the church, which is His body, the fullness of Him who fills all in all.

In whom we have redemption through His blood, the forgiveness of sins, according to the riches of His grace

Ephesians 1:7

CHAPTER 9

MEDITATION STATIONS

Here we are! We have walked through some key ways to incorporate meditation into our lifestyles. Here is what I promised you; this is what Holy Spirit gave me for our women's weekend away. Try one or try them all, 30-45 minute stations. I hope this inspires you to come up with your own creative ways to set up opportunities for relaxation and meditation.

Many women struggle to sit for even five minutes in silence. But I encourage you to start off with five minutes and build yourself up. It does get easier and your body needs that rest. What we do spiritually blesses our physical and the physical blesses the spiritual. They go hand in hand.

First things first. Ask yourself, "Do I believe this book is a sound biblical tool to help me on my journey with Jesus? How can I apply what I'm reading and learning from this book? How much of this book has given me a lightbulb moment to think, *Oh, I really need to do this!* Have I seen the value in meditation? Do I understand it is a necessity, not an option? Do I recognize how the enemy sets spiritual traps to keep me from my relationship with Jesus?" After you ask yourself some foundational questions, set some action steps for yourself. Your time is now. Get started!

The Meditation Stations were the main part of our weekend revival. They were designed to help the women understand themselves, see where they were and where they wanted to be, and to provide action steps to help them get there in their relationship with Jesus. I encouraged them to disconnect from life, turn their phones off, and just be with the Lord.

We started our weekend journaling in our *Dear God* journals. Our first entry was:

- What are you expecting from your weekend retreat?
- How do you want God to meet you?

We took the time to journal before and after each session, just to get a gauge of our hearts and minds. This is vitally important to help us learn. We do a lot of thinking, unaware that our minds keep running. Intentionally controlling our thought life can help us maximize whatever it is we are preparing for.

Here is the flow of our Saturday afternoon and the stations I assigned:

Station 1 - Soaking to Be Still and Silent

This is the most important station. The importance of this station is for you to get to know yourself when you are alone in silence.

- What does your mind want to wonder off with?
- Are you restless?
- What consumes your thoughts?
- What struggles surface when you are still and silent?
- Does God talk with you or do you do all the talking?

Journal before and after this station. Questions to answer in your *Dear God* journal:

- What do I really think of this exercise?
- How does it make me feel to think I have to sit still and be in silence for 30 minutes?
- What do I hope to receive by doing this?

- What do I think this exercise will show me?
- Who am I?
- Who do I really want to be?
- What is my relationship with God like?
- Are my heart and mind consumed with Jesus, myself, others, or things?
- Am I capable of just *being* or do I always feel the need to *do*?

Of course, if the Lord gives you any other insight, write it down.

Station 2 - Soaking in Instrumental Worship Music

I believe this station is the gateway to allowing ourselves to relax. It quiets our minds. As you soak in the music, picture yourself sitting on the Father's lap. Envision being with Him. Think good thoughts, lovely thoughts. Think of memories that brought you great joy. If a condemning thought or anything negative comes to mind, refuse it in Jesus' name.

Philippians 4:8 - "Finally, brethren, whatever is true, whatever is honorable, whatever is right, whatever is pure, whatever is lovely, whatever is of good repute, if there is any excellence and if anything worthy of praise, dwell on these things."

Now we will just soak in the sounds of the instruments that are bringing a lovely sound to hymns of our hearts.

Journal immediately following. Questions to answer in your *Dear God* journal:

- How did you feel soaking in the music?
- What were your thoughts like?
- What came to your mind?
- Did you experience a battle?
- How did you handle that battle?
- Did you envision anything in your mind's eye?
- Are you starting to see the benefit of being still?

Station 3 - Soaking in Scripture Reading

This station is extremely vital to soak in God's Word. Once we have come to learn our minds and what controls our thoughts, we can prepare for a change. By allowing the Word to wash over us, we can intentionally fix our thoughts on the Scriptures.

During this station, we soaked in Scripture readings with our eye masks on. I suggest you search YouTube for videos of peace verses. We are bringing peace to mind.

Journal immediately after this. Questions to answer in your *Dear God* journal:

- What was your expectation of yourself while sitting through Scripture reading?
- Did you do what you thought you expected?
- How did just relaxing and soaking in the Living Word impact you?
- Were you able to relax?
- Did you feel uneasy and restless?
- Did you ask yourself when will this be over?
- Are you hearing the voice of the Lord?

Whatever the Lord revealed to you—good, bad, ugly—journal it.

Station 4 - Creating in Creation with the Creator with instrumental birdsongs

Use art supplies to journal a **Life Map for God** on poster board with your creative mind. Your life map is individual. It's yours. It might look like any number of things. Your life map might demonstrate where you've been, where you are now, and where you want to be. Or you might like to try your hand at drawing a tree in your backyard, or another scene from the nature around you. However, the Holy Spirit may lay something else on your mind for you to create. This is an opportunity to sit still, to hear from God, and to allow Him to give you a visual of what He wants to communicate to you. Many of us went into this exercise expecting one thing and found that God had something entirely different in mind.

I personally went in thinking I was going to draw a picture of the bay. But as I got started, God prompted me to reflect on my salvation story and put it into pictures. It was a very emotional time as God conveyed His heart for me. It was as if the Holy Spirit came together with my heart and my mind, and it flowed onto my poster board.

This is what my final product looked like: the Holy Spirit had me draw a visual of the burden of what felt like five elephants on my shoulders. I was chained to them. This was before I came to Christ. Next, I drew a tombstone with my name on it. I was the walking dead before I knew Him. After I gave Him my heart, the chains and burdens fell from my shoulders. I was made alive, and I busted out of the grave! I've been living for Him ever since. Spiritually, I had given Jesus my heart with one hand. He took my other hand and walked me into the light. I added this to my poster board. This imagery represents exactly what happened. He set me free from the bondage of sin that weighed me down. Next, He had me draw a picture of myself in a wedding dress, waiting for His return. That's the story of my life. I live for His return!

This is a personalized *Life Map for God—just you and God*. This afternoon has been a pause in your life where you think only of Him, no one else. Don't be intimidated by whether or not you can actually create a masterpiece. Use this time to be creative. Depict what is going on in your life and allow that to flow in living color onto the pallet we call *Your Story*. This is where you can let go of some unpleasant memories. You can right your wrongs by identifying them, confessing them and giving them over to the Lord. There are things that are holding you back from a deeper, more intimate relationship with Him, aren't there? I encourage you to see just how good He is to you and for you, and start creating the life you desire to live. It starts here. Your time is now!

You may want to play an instrumental piece with nature sounds in the background. YouTube is a good resource. Allow the sound of the songbirds, His beautiful creation, to resonate in your heart with great peace and joy. Every time they sing, they sing His praises. They know who they belong to, and they are making a joyful noise unto their

Creator. Allow their simplicity to inspire something of great significance in you as you allow your mind, heart, and hands to draw out your *Life Map for God.* There is no right or wrong. It's individual, unique, and one of a kind—just like you. A pearl of great price. God uses our trials like sandpaper to smooth out the rough edges. This will smooth your heart and bring a brilliant luster and shine for His glory. He is preparing a beautiful bride without spot or wrinkle who awaits her Bridegroom. He is coming! We must be intentional and ready.

Be Free, Be YOU, Just BE!

This one is all you. Write in your *Dear God* journal.

- Share your heart.
- Express your gratefulness.
- Praise Him for His goodness.
- How did your Life Map for God bring a new level of awareness of your relationship with Him?

Station 5 - Prayer Walk, Thankful Walk, Prayer Room Stations

This station invites you to go into the created world, take in the beautiful handiwork of our amazing Creator, and commune with Him and Him alone. Please do not skip this last and vital station. God is worthy of your praises. He is worthy of your undivided attention and gratitude. There are going to be things you need to talk to Him about after the last four stations. This is your time to make that happen. Take a walk in the park, the woods, or on your street.

Being in God's presence is so precious and a busy, noisy world robs us of this pleasure. Take in what you are seeing around you. Don't just see it, take it in. "Stop to smell the roses."

Just in case you're not sure what to say or do, I provided two chapters out of Psalms that you can read to Him. While you read them, read with thanksgiving, believing them for yourself.

Enjoy your time with Daddy.

As the Holy Spirit has downloaded this to me to share with you, I am praying and fasting for your understanding of "Be still and know that I am God."

Psalm 16
Preserve me, O God, for I take refuge in You.
I said to the Lord, "You are my Lord;
I have no good besides You."
As for the saints who are in the earth,
They are the majestic ones in whom is all my delight.
The sorrows of those who have bartered for an-
other God will be multiplied;
I shall not pour out their drink offerings of blood,
Nor will I take their names upon my lips.
The Lord is the portion of my inheritance and my cup;
You support my lot.
The lines have fallen to me in pleasant places;
Indeed, my heritage is beautiful to me.
I will bless the Lord who has counseled me;
Indeed, my mind instructs me in the night.
I have set the Lord continually before me;
Because He is at my right hand, I will not be shaken.
Therefore my heart is glad and my glory rejoices;
My flesh also will dwell securely.
For You will not abandon my soul to Sheol;
Nor will You allow Your Holy One to undergo decay.
You will make known to me the path of life;
In Your presence is fullness of joy; In Your
right hand there are pleasures forever.

Psalm 23
The Lord is my shepherd,
I shall not want.

He makes me lie down in green pastures;
He leads me beside quiet waters.
He restores my soul;
He guides me in the paths of righteousness
For His name's sake.
Even though I walk through the val-
ley of the shadow of death,
I fear no evil, for You are with me;
Your rod and Your staff, they comfort me.
You prepare a table before me in the presence of my enemies;
You have anointed my head with oil;
My cup overflows.
Surely goodness and lovingkindness will fol-
low me all the days of my life,
And I will dwell in the house of the Lord forever.

Reviews of Meditation Stations

Each woman who completed the Meditation Stations said taking a whole afternoon going through the stations was one of the best things she's ever done. Here are comments from some of the women after spending the afternoon meditating:

> I have been away on many women's weekend retreats through the years. I have never been more satisfied with my time away as this weekend! This was by far the best experience I have ever had being intentional with the Lord. The meditation stations where the perfect tool to help me see how much time I give away to everything else other than God. My favorite station was listening to the Word of God being read over me. I also enjoyed walking in creation, practicing His presence, and giving thanks for a relaxing and spiritually uplifting afternoon. I can't wait for the next one!   ~ DH

By blocking out all distractions I became alone with God. Each phase brought a closeness to God and prepared me to wholly be one with Him. When it was over I left renewed in His love and was filled with the Spirit. Wanting to love God with all of me. So thankful for this experience. ~ NG

I found that spending an entire afternoon sitting in God's presence, relaxing and taking in His Word was one of the most satisfying afternoons I've had in a long time. It was such a blessing. I loved the 30-minute walk in nature. It was the best women's weekend afternoon I've ever had! ~ DM

I found that all I could say over and over after my walk with God was, Thank you, thank you, thank you. I needed that afternoon set apart for Him, I needed to be with HIM! I came needy and finished filled, so filled! ~ DM

I liked the station that I was soaking in the Scriptures of peace. It confirmed how the Word is so crucial in our lives to have my mind renewed. What I got out of our quiet time was how important it is to listen. No noise was crucial to hearing the Lord's voice. ~ HV

1st station, God spoke to me through the quiet time, where I was totally focused on him. The 5th station when I took a walk, as I came out the doors there was a cloud with sunbeams coming down to the earth, I felt God was confirming to me what He had spoken to me in my heart. Additionally, I did not know what to expect when I got there, but wow! ~ PJ

Well, I had no idea what I was in for, plus all the new faces...But I must say it was an awesome weekend learning how to listen. To be in silence is hard but so needed. I didn't like the total silent session because my mind just wandered *everywhere*. But the one that we had the light music playing in the background, made me feel so peaceful and opened my thought as to what God was trying to say to me. Even though I may have a plate full in life, He is there with me if I just let Him and stop thinking I can do all things on my own. Once I felt that strong feeling I had so much peace I think I dozed off. Oops! So I would definitely say that was my moment. Again, the whole weekend was just an awesome experience. ~ LP

Taking an afternoon to be still in the presence of God was so necessary. My mind is always busy thinking about things that need to be done now, a month from now, six months from now—and things that should have been done yesterday. Entering into the meditation stations, I purposed to leave everything at the door and focus my attention on my time with Jesus. God met me there in a powerful way. "Creating with the Creator" was the station that impacted me the most. The Holy Spirit used the project to answer an important question I had been praying about. ~ JM

I honestly wasn't sure what to expect but I knew God was going to do something special and good for my spiritual growth. I just allowed the Lord to relax me in such a way that I was able to focus on Him completely with no distractions. God took me away from home and placed me in complete quietness. In the beginning of the first session, I had to rebuke Satan as he was causing confusion and distraction. I prayed and asked God in the name of Jesus Christ of Nazareth to remove Satan, his minions, cohorts, and demons. I enjoyed every station. I was able to think out what God was trying to show me in the drawing session. He clearly gave me the picture of myself sitting backward to family and looking forward to Him and only Him because He is all I need. My family will see and follow me as I follow Christ or they will not. The choice is theirs, but my focus must stay on Jesus. I enjoyed the music and the Bible reading sessions too. ~ GR

Thank you for this weekend. It was amazing. I was hesitant to attend because of my insecurities and feelings of not belonging. The meditation stations were life changing. God showed me exactly what I have needed and longed for my entire life. ~ AG

I didn't know what to expect. I came last minute, I hadn't known the theme of the weekend. I just kept asking God to let me know more of Him and to revive me! He certainly did! Meditation beginning with 30 minutes of silence then journaling. As I continued the Lord just said, "I love you." As our last session of meditation, we walked in silence outdoors. I stood in front of the water and the sun glistened on the water with a glare from the sun. I found myself wanting to move towards the shade. Then God spoke to me and said, "Stand in the light." I stood in the sun and the warmth filled me and gave me a relaxation of Agape love. ~ JK

The "Be Still" Retreat was a time of refreshment for me. Setting time aside to stop and rest in the presence of God was something I had been desiring to do for a while. The meditation station that spoke to me the most was the Scripture readings. Every Scripture that was read over me reminded me of God's provision, faithfulness, and promises. He reminded me how His Word has been living and active throughout my life and how it is important for me to break away from my busy schedule and be intentional about getting away with Him. ~ IC

EXPOSING A RELIGIOUS SPIRIT

There is a great divide among God's people. The body of Christ, the Church, battles against itself. This should not be!

Scripture encourages us to love one another, to prefer one another over ourselves, to lay one's life down for another. But love seems to be the furthest thing from the minds of many, if the other person does not conform to their exact beliefs. We live in a world where people want what they want—when they want it. And if you don't think like I think, act like I act, or say what I say—you're out! The fight is on.

Self-righteousness is the result of the spiritual trap of a religious spirit. Our Father, God of the Universe, Jesus the Son of God, and Holy Spirit never, ever, not even for one minute invented, created, or manufactured "religion." It is completely man-made.

Genesis 11 tells the story of Nimrod. He was Noah's great-grandson, a descendant of Ham. Nimrod in the Hebrew means "a warrior against God." He wanted to build a tower to heaven—a man-made bridge from earth to heaven. As if he wanted to literally work his way to the heavens.

If you notice, religious spirits want us to stay stuck in doing, attempting to manufacture our own results. They cause us to burn out in performance. This comes from a mindset of striving in our own strength. We often feel a sense of accomplishment in our striving. How often has that striving left you feeling as if you still missed the boat, insecure in your efforts, rejected for not excelling, and so on? You don't see him behind the scenes, but this is the work of the enemy trying to distract and destroy you. He is orchestrating your demise. If he can keep you operating in your own strength or ability, you will never think to include God in your efforts.

A healthy relationship with God is a joint, proactive, intentional exchange. It's complete dependence on Him for all of your needs, even when He gives you the permission to achieve all that you desire.

There are many ways that a religious spirit can sneak into our hearts and capture our right minds into wrong thinking. We should be mindful of our hearts and what we allow to overtake us. Legalism and perfectionism are great dividers of the Body of Christ. They can cause intolerance, condemnation, and great confusion among believers.

Here are some signs of a religious spirit:

- Critical spirit: you are critical of how others relate to God
- Judgmental spirit: you judge those you feel do not measure up to your religious standard
- You try to work for your salvation
- You desire busyness in activities rather than a stillness in your relationship with the Lord
- You prefer performance over presence
- Your identity is based on what you do, rather than who you belong to
- You expel doctrine but don't understand the message
- You speak holiness but walk without inward transformation

These tendencies wage war against the beauty of God's love and grace. In Scripture, we see this demonstrated by the Pharisees. These men, with no understanding of God's love and grace, continually projected religion onto others. Jesus disapproved of this religious spirit and constantly challenged the mindset of the Pharisees.

Pause: This is a time for reflection and meditation. Do you feel as though God is far away? Ask the Holy Spirit to reveal if there is anything distracting you from walking closely with the Lord.

Remember, Scriptures tell us there is no condemnation to those who are in Christ Jesus. It's important to renew your mind daily to overcome the lies that can easily beset us. If you struggle with any of these symptoms, you're not alone. We all struggle with a religious spirit, or have at one time. I offer you a way to release these and be in right standing with your God.

1. Identify your particular struggle.
2. Confess it as a lie, and that it is counter-intuitive to the Lord's desire for you.
3. Ask for forgiveness and place yourself in alignment with the word of God.
4. Speak out loud and rebuke the spirit that has come up against you to steal, kill, and destroy. Cut it off in the spiritual realm. Declare that you are a child of God. Trust that you are forgiven and it no longer has any rights or jurisdiction over you.

This new understanding will help you be aware of how you relate to others. If you identify with any of the symptoms we mentioned, take immediate action. Identify negative thoughts. Replace them with positive reinforcement by reading, out loud, the promises of God found in Scriptures. Here are a few to help you get started.

- All things work together for good to them that love God, to them who are the called according to HIS purpose. (Romans 8:28)
- For God hath not given me the spirit of fear; but of power, love, and of a sound mind. (2 Timothy 1:7)
- He will keep me in perfect peace, whose mind is stayed on thee: because I trust in thee. (Isaiah 26:3)
- No weapon that is formed against thee shall prosper; This [is] the heritage of the servants of the LORD, and their righteousness [is] of me, saith the LORD. (Isaiah 54:17 a, c)
- Don't fear; for I am with thee: be not dismayed; for I am your God: I will strengthen you; yes, I will help you; yes, I will

uphold you with the right hand of my righteousness. (Isaiah 41:10)
- For the Lord will be MY confidence and will keep MY foot from being snared! (Proverbs 3:26)
- The Lord MY God will continually guide ME! (Isaiah 58:11)
- I AM confident; the Lord began a good work in ME and will continue to perform it. (Philippians 1:6)
- It is God that works in ME to will and do of His good pleasure! (Philippians 2:13)

If you are struggling and need help walking through this process, please do not hesitate to look me up on Facebook. Instant message me, I would be happy to help you!

I love people and desire for them to live a fulfilled satisfying spiritual life in Christ. Abundance is what we are offered. It is my passion to help you achieve that!

Your friend,

Debbie Mascioli

CONCLUSION

We put oil in oil lamps to produce light. We put gas in our cars so we can get to where we need to go. Cars and oil lamps, each designed for a particular purpose, require specific fuel to fulfill their function. Without frequently filling them up, they will not work properly.

Remember the void we talked about and how we are always trying to fill it? Trying to live outside of God is fleeting and exhausting. Trying to produce results without His "filling" is like trying to drive a car without gas. Do you see the point being made here? It is impossible to do what we have been created to do without being filled.

Humans were created for a specific purpose. Isaiah 43:7 tells us that we were created to glorify God! John 14:16 tells us, "And I will ask the Father, and he will give you another Advocate, who will never leave you." We require a certain filling—The Holy Spirit. We cannot be any closer to God than when He has taken up residence within us! He is with us, for us, and in us! Do you remember what I shared about my visit to the Western Wall? Because the Holy Spirit occupies us, we don't need to go far to be close to God.

What do we as humans need to be functional? The Gospel. Jesus Christ. The Holy Spirit. Jesus and the Gospel are not just a ticket to heaven. Jesus came with power for many reasons. Let's highlight a few of those reasons:

- To set us free from sin and death.
- To leave us His advocate, our Helper, our Comforter . . . so that we can live out His Kingdom agenda here on earth. Without the

111

Holy Spirit we cannot walk closely with Him. The Holy Spirit is for us as gas is to a car. He gives us what we need to function as we were created.

- That we represent the Father in holiness and righteousness in order to glorify Him.
- That we love others as He has loved us.
- That we allow Him to live in and through us by the power of the Holy Spirit.
- That we may one day live with Him in eternity.
- That we will reign with Him.

Thus the unfolding of the secret—the answer to why we have this void and feel so far away from God. Have you recognized the importance of your filling throughout this personal practical guide?

When we come to realize that we feel far away from God, James 4:7,8 gives us action steps to draw closer to Him:

- Submit and humble yourself before God: Assess where you are with Him.
- Resist the devil: Identify spiritual traps and make any necessary changes in your life to draw closer to God.
- Draw near to God, and He will draw near to you: Be intentional to apply these biblical principles on meditation to your life.
- Wash your hands and purify your heart: Accept the Gospel and repent of sin daily.
- Examine yourself: Where does your loyalty lie? Is it divided between God and the busyness of the world? Remember meditation is a necessity, not an option!

I pray that this book will be a tool used for God's glory in your life. May God's people be awakened to the "more" they can have with Him.

Your Time is Now!
Esther 4:14b

PRAISE FOR *WHEN GOD FEELS FAR AWAY*

"I am pleased that there is a message which encourages from the scripture that meditating is a Christian practice and not simply a religious movement! I have come away with a stronger understanding of how to grow my relationship with God specifically through Debbie's personal examples. This text gives scripture-related clarity and therefore should help enhance one's communication with God."

~ Andrea Hampton
Sandy Cove Women's Ministry Coordinator

If you've ever hungered for more out of the Christian life, longed for a deeper walk, or wondered where is God in the crazy world this book is for you. Debbie Mascioli takes you by the hand and leads you on a personal retreat. Her personal story and practical teaching will give you a fresh look at ancient practices to help you live a life available to all but so few discover.

~ Gordon Douglas
Christian comedian, pastor, author,
inspirational speaker

"What a great topic! Thank you for bringing it to the forefront. I love Debbie Mascioli's book because I know and love Debbie . . . much like I love the Bible because I know and love Jesus! Knowing and loving the author gives great credence to what is written. Debbie lives and practices what she writes. Read and learn proven, and perhaps neglected, tools to draw closer to the Lord and thereby advance in the process of being transformed by the renewing of your mind."

~ Candy Davison
Sandy Cove Women's Ministry Coordinator Emeritus

"What an incredible handbook for creating a changed life! The words on these pages may well turn your life upside down spiritually . . . in the most exhilarating, transformational way! You will discover a life-changing secret for how to experience the supernatural reality of a meaningful life in Christ. No more need to chase every new idea for "how to be a better Christian." No . . . you will find the unique way in which God is speaking just to you, drawing you closer to Him and teaching you of Himself. Expect to be revolutionized through personal Holy Spirit revelation."

~ Glenna Salsbury
Professional Speaker
Author of *The Art of the Fresh Start*
CSP, CPAE Speaker Hall of Fame

"When you sit under Debbie's teaching, you will find someone who is excited about what Jesus is doing in her life. Her desire to encourage others in their journey with Jesus is obvious as she invites us to taste and see for ourselves just how good the Lord really is. It's evident that God has gifted Debbie to encourage the potential in others and empower them to fulfill their purpose. She demonstrates from personal experience what our lives can look like when we take hold of the Word of God and use it in the way Jesus instructed, 'Be doers of the Word and not hearers only.'"

~ Jennifer Muller
Whole Heart Ministries

ABOUT THE AUTHOR

Debbie is an authentic, down-to-earth Jesus follower who genuinely loves others, sees their full potential and desires to empower them to live the abundant life. Her enthusiasm and energy for Jesus is contagious. She has a way of bringing the Scriptures alive, making them understandable to us all. Because of her own transformation, Debbie is passionate and intentional about sharing the truths of God's Word and challenging others to *believe* and live for Jesus. She shares her God stories with the hope they will inspire others to know that God is not only real, but alive, active, and moving on our behalf.

Debbie, an executive director on the John Maxwell team, is certified as a coach, speaker, and trainer. She is a Christian conciliator, mediator, and conflict coach through Peacemaker University. Debbie is an entrepreneur, founder of a nonprofit women's ministry, and an international speaker. She has also published a Christian women's magazine.

Married to her soulmate, Pastor Sammy, she has been coaching, counseling, mentoring, and discipling women for 25 years. She is a mom to four amazing young people whom she adores, an energetic, loyal friend to many, and a loving author to her readers. She and her family enjoy the beach, camping, and being outdoors together.

To hire Debbie for coaching or speaking, please contact her at www. debbiemascioli.com.

89888676R00074

Made in the USA
Columbia, SC
22 February 2018